The Secret to Political Happiness

dynamicauthority@gmail.com

www.politicalhappiness.com

Ramsey Angus Malcolm,
 1950-

The secret to Political Happiness.

Cdn ISBN 978 0992077501

ISBN-13:978-1453768105

ISBN-10:1453768106

If you have lost faith in the political system

You are not alone!

Western society has used representative democracy for two hundred years without an update or upgrade. Our ancient democracy is failing to address pressing problems of climate change, economic and social instability, and a growing frustration as citizen's liberty evaporates. Many of these problems are being temporarily solved by massive debt which has been enabled through the sinister interests of money. We are moving from a democracy to a plutocracy. There is no historical precedent to measure the consequences of plutocracy, however there is a precedent showing the benefits of updating democracy.

Cover photo

The cover is a photograph of a peace rose in full bloom. The delicate structures and brilliant colors adorned with tiny drops of dew show the magic and power of the environment we share. To grow a perfect rose takes a perfect set of circumstances.

The human species can be compared to a rose struggling to survive on rocky and hostile territory. Over millenniums we have sprouted buds of understanding, developing flowers of peace and prosperity ready to burst into bloom. The human species has never had a chance to achieve full bloom. Our own people have nipped the buds with autocracy and covered the entire plant of humanity with the black rust of oppression. For whatever reason, the buds have fallen, never allowing the true colors of the human-race to shine through.

Today we have a near perfect set of circumstances to allow humankind to expose her true gentle nature. All we need is a tiny drop of fertilizer in the form of understanding to allow the brilliance and intricate structures of the human family to burst into a bloom of peace and prosperity.

Index

Prologue

As a young man I lived in a world filled with the madness of war on the brink of a nuclear holocaust. I had a dream.
I dreamed that when I was old I would be living in a world free of war, corruption and oppression. I dreamed I would be living on a planet where a peaceful human race shares the bounty of our planet with all life forms.
Now I am old. I share an amazing world enhanced by technology but my dream of border crossings dissolving into welcome centers filled with people who have a deep trust in one another has not occurred. Instead I live in a world filled with the madness of war on the brink of nuclear holocaust run by madmen.
As an old man I want to pass on the dream of peace and justice to a new generation.

A society grows great when old men plant trees whose shade they know they shall not sit in? Greek proverb

Time Line

Birth: I was overjoyed to be here. For the first six years I lived on an isolated fruit farm in the Similkameen Valley of British Columbia. I had bad eye-sight, but I vividly remember the perfume of sagebrush and an orchestra of rhythmic insects chirping in the hundred plus temperatures of summer.

Formative years: With thick glasses I could see. Transplanted to the Cowichan Valley of Vancouver Island, I was influenced by First Nations, Chinese, East Indian and many immigrant European cultures.

Childhood: I learned how physical things worked; human inventions, internal combustion engines, electrical circuits and model aircraft, became my passion. I could understand their complexities and fix almost anything. In my childhood I became a devout member of our local library. I found books and received a lot of good advice from the librarians who helped me find information about difficult subjects like astronomy, aerodynamics and how radios work.

Youth: Politicians seemed to exist in a mysterious world, far above my existence, eluding me. I knew nothing of the importance of politics. I really didn't care. I was still alive after a narrow miss with nuclear war in the early sixties. I was exposed to many interesting philosophies in the rebellious sixties while indulging in cool drugs living without forethought as a free thinker in the world of my ancestors.

Career: I discovered a place where I was needed.

Family: I found a wonderful wife, or did she find me? We had two children.

Awareness: One day my librarian directed me to a retired electrical engineer who taught ham radio. Soon I was communicating in Morse code where there are no borders. Russians told me, in great detail, how superior their communist world was, trying to fill me with their propaganda. The French talked of their food and how they had the best wine. The Japanese explained the significance and beauty of their cherry blossom festivals and the Americans talked a lot about the weather. As my understanding of the natural world expanded I worried about the future of my children.

Then I ran headlong into something I couldn't understand. How could politicians be so stupid? My understanding told me politicians were God like. I believed these people existed in some secret dimension where they made decisions with reasons I couldn't understand. After all they had prevented the impending nuclear holocaust when I was in my early teens. But, I questioned why were politicians stupid enough to get into a quagmire where one step in the wrong direction could end all life on earth in a nuclear war.

I watched the east coast cod industry die. I watched the west coast salmon industries dwindle. I watched as good high tech jobs were exported. I watched our national debt grow at nerve racking speed. I watched as we desperately extracted our precious natural resources and shipped them out of the country. I watched as our bureaucracies grew and felt their tightening noose of oppression. And like the captain of a sinking ship saying, "don't worry, we aren't sinking," I watched politicians lie about what a wonderful job they were doing.

I did what I had always done when I didn't understand. I asked a librarian. This was BG (Before Google).

I was started on an introductory diet of politics. Over the next ten years reading politics became a passion. I went on a journey of discovery, reading backwards from the present through American and Canadian political history searching for a common link between political theories. My intellectual journey took me across the Atlantic as I read about the French revolution, the Bolshevik revolution, the monarchies, the English Parliament, the intrigue of Oliver Cromwell, the struggle for franchise with the suffrage movement but still there was no revelation. I leapt over the medieval period and into antiquities.

I remember the day a wave of understanding finally washed over me. Our public library phoned and said they had found a book I had requested nine months earlier. This was a surprise because I had been told it was unavailable, last printed in 1946, written in three hundred BC by Aristotle, called "Politics".

The librarian said I could only keep it for one week because they had borrowed it from the St. Michael's Boys School in Victoria. I picked it up on my way to attending a convention in Vancouver with the thought I would read it between sessions.

The book was translated from the original Greek and heavily annotated with interpretations of the original text. Between the lines I managed to find this simple thought: **All men want to be able to go about their business (lives) without interference. When people go about their business they interfere with each other. This interference in the absence of law ultimately leads to war, murder, rape and pillage. Politics has the power to stop the harm done from this interference by making laws. To make laws one needs a source of authority. Legitimate laws made by a consensus of citizens are the only laws that are not oppressive. The ancient Greeks had stopped tyranny by uniting their nation through the political equality of their citizens. What a noble thought!**

I remember guiltily reading in the conference hall, hiding my dusty old book between the covers of the glossy conference cover ignoring the speeches. Feeling a bit stupid I looked up at the people around me. At the time it seemed obvious, everyone already knew this simple truth but no-one had bothered to tell me. I was afraid to ask, but soon found I was alone in my understanding.

This understanding clarified much of the history I had previously read. I continued reading filling in the blanks and reading again to consolidate my new understanding. Everything made perfect sense. I became very excited, realizing with this new understanding, there is a simple cure to the problems we are having in our modern world.

My vision was so clear I couldn't imagine the rest of the world not celebrating the beginning of a new era. I had meetings and gained enough support to run as an independent candidate for our provincial legislature. I worked hard and managed to gain some votes.

I also gained insight. I felt like an eleventh century intellectual who had realized the earth was not flat but in fact round and the sun did not revolve around us. I tried to convince my would-be constituents that the citizen is the center of a round political world with politicians revolving around the citizen, not the other way around. The idea didn't go over well. The idea was too foreign. Many people who responded tried to slot my political theory into a known political ideology.

People have said I sound like an American. I have been called a Communist, a Capitalist, a Socialist, a Libertarian, a Scientologist, a Conservative, a left-wing bleeding-heart liberal and even a Republican. It seems I am the opposite of everyone's political stripe. I believe the biggest sentiments obstructing political progress is a fear of change from those who hold power and a population indoctrinated with an out of date, old and tired system of representative democracy.

The sentiment "don't mess with stuff you don't know anything about" was very clear. I took the advice of many of my friends, concentrating my energy on my work, building houses and boats and I stayed as far away from politics as possible.

Retirement: My wife and I sailed off in a boat I had built. I had time on my hands and decided I should try to write. I found I enjoyed writing but, like politics, I discovered that writing well is not something that comes naturally to me.

I wrote a number of novels and figured out how to enjoy my hobby at very little cost. In 2009 I tried writing a serious book about what I consider modern participative democracy.

I tossed it aside and now in 2017 I have decided to try again. I hope these musings make sense.

I write this because I can't see how exposing the gentle side of humanity can do any harm ("Primum non nocere" first do no harm). I am hoping these notes will plant seeds in the minds of our younger more capable citizens who perhaps will change this beautiful imagined reality into an enduring political construct.

This writing is **not only** about the politics of making law. Every aspect of life, including the family, the work/place or relationships within a group can be improved with these simple understandings. A fundamental savvy of politics is priceless spanning the entire spectrum of the humanity.

My perspective has changed from one of fear and mistrust, in my fellow men, to a love fest where the people around me have become precious gems of uniqueness. My trust has not gone unrewarded. I now have deep friendships with people all over the world. When I look at people, I see a set of traits planted by their ancestors (nature) mixed with a set of beliefs planted by their environment (nurture). Democratic society is exposing the beautiful side of humanity. As more of us see the beauty in our fellow citizens we will use our equality to make law and move towards a happy future.

This is not an academic work. My list of references is incomplete because I have not referenced my observations and have not documented many of the books that I have borrowed from the library. You might be offended by my unsubstantiated observation such as people who are oppressed don't smile or laugh as much as people who live in an environment of liberty. I may be wrong and if I am I want you to correct me and use your mind to find a better way to fix the problems we collectively face. A journey of a thousand miles begins with a single step.

Chapter 1   *The Discussion*

Blessed are the meek: for they shall inherit the earth.   Mathew 5: 5

In the watery vision of my life I wonder if it matters who you are. What color is your skin, are you a man, a woman or perhaps a person of indeterminate sex. No matter what ideologies you have picked up in your life, I believe every person is important and has a role to play in making our world a better place. *Because we exist we are politically equal.*

In a democracy, each citizen controls exactly the same amount of political authority (Piece of Political Authority POPA), from the age of consent until the end of life. Each human, who lives today, has around sixty-thousand generations of human genus ancestors. Each person, with a heart beating in their chest has inherited, from their ancestors, the gift of planetary citizenship. It is no different than inheriting your granny's car or inheriting millions of dollars from your parents. The citizen controls what they do with their inheritance. This inherited piece of political authority can be used to make **law** or a citizen can relax and simply live with laws others have instituted.

No one can dispute the fact that human beings in western society live better today than at any time in history. Is this because we suddenly realized how to withdraw natural resources (coal, gas and oil) deposited millions of years ago? And like a bank account, with seemingly unlimited resources, will we squander and deplete our future? Or is it because **we have discovered something beautiful about human beings**? How many of the people in western society have the foggiest idea of how western society achieved our present splendor?

Like math, are there some fundamental principles we can easily learn to give meaning to our politics? Do we realize how important our political ideologies are and how they relate to the quality of our lives?

It would be a horrible twist to lose our present splendor because of our ignorance. I realize there are as many solutions to political problems as there are people participating in any political discussion. Before we begin we should think hard about what we really want. What is more important, the personalities and foibles of our elected people or the actual laws make by our law makers? No one can answer with certainty the question: where did we come from? What are we doing here? And where are we going? However, to siting like frogs in a pot of warming water, ignoring what is happening around us, will not cure our problems.

At the beginning of the twenty-first century everyone knows that Western Society's political system is old, tired and needs replacing. We can compare our two hundred year old representative democracy to a horse and buggy going down a busy freeway. For safety reasons we need an army of police cars to protect our old political buggy. Although the politicians riding in the buggy are doing their best they are obstructing progress and they are a danger to themselves and the people around them.

The authority of our representative governments is being eroded. To make laws governments are increasingly asking permission from a growing system of plutocracy. It is ironic to see the cradle of our modern world (Greece) is one of the first to accept, under protest, plutocracy as the source of authority to make law. Most representative democracies are not far behind.

It is impossible to know which source of authority will replace our representative democracies. We may fall into the trap of autocracy with the likes of Donald Trump of the USA and Rob Ford of Toronto. The stock market growth after the election of Trump is an indicator of who is benefiting from a more autocratic government. Or we can recognize and capture the powerful authority of our citizens. Theodore Roosevelt: "The majority of the plain people will day in and day out make fewer mistakes in governing themselves than any smaller body of men will make trying to govern them."

People living in western society beyond the third decade of life have been indoctrinated with our present system of government and have a heavy prejudice and fear of political change. This prejudice and fear stands in the way of political progress and leaves the enlightened and the young, who are not fettered with this burden, to move forward.

I am confident there are many options for future political models that don't increase autocracy. I have tried to present good arguments supporting less autocracy with a plan to gently migrate our governments towards a more participative model.

If my understanding is correct the benefits of participative democracy are ***beyond belief***. I am confident that, if any person, rich or poor, is given an opportunity to live in a world governed by participative democracy they would never want to go back to our present system of representative democracy.

Finding a way to convince a few influential people that these principles are ***not beyond belief***, and are in fact a natural state, is the first challenge.

1920 Women's suffrage expands the democratic foundation in western society creating an amazing world of undreamed of wealth, liberty and security for the majority. This political change also resulted in smaller families and declining population growth for this group of people.

2020 Massive wealth and power is accumulated by a minority of privileged individuals. Contractual agreements held by plutocrats restrict democratic sovereignty. Massive accumulated debt enslaves the majority creating anger, frustration and political unhappiness (modern Greece). Citizens see the light and use technology to update democracy and regain their sovereignty. Just as the political change resulting from the suffrage movement at the beginning of the twentieth century produced unbelievable unexpected benefits so too will the political shift at the beginning of the twenty first century produce unbelievable liberty, stability and political happiness for the majority.

In the year 2117 you wake at seven after a busy night watching the results of an election. Your candidate didn't win. You find your device, check your emails, catch up on some Facebook chatter, maybe check your bank account and move some money into your checking account. Then you open your political account. You note who is using your POPA at your municipal level, state or provincial level, federal level and UN level. You go through the list of winners of the political contest from the night before. You move your POPA to a winning candidate who represents your interests, close your political account and then enjoy your four hour work day. You have lots of time with friends to discuss issues and find information about new laws that are being proposed by your elected officials. By the end of the day after being influenced by your friends and doing a bit of snooping you may want to change which politician is using your POPA.

Chapter 2 *The Logic*

What is politics and why is it the most important part of establishing the quality of our lives?

→ The basic premise is that all people want to go about their business (their lives) without interference.

→ When people go about their business they interfere with each other.

→ In the past this **interference**, in the absence of **law**, ultimately lead to war, murder, rape and pillage.

→ **Law** is a magic spice that prevents people from doing harm to each other.

If legitimate **Law** is a magic spice that, when sprinkled over human beings, stops the negative side of humanity, where do we find it? It's not a good idea to search through jungles or in exotic places far away from civilization. A more sensible approach is to look to our past. Our history books tell us we can make our own law with one essential ingredient, a **source of authority**. The most popular source of authority, historically has been the individual; King, Queen, Shah, Tsar, Sultan, Emperor, Monarch, Pharaoh, dictator, autocrat chief, Meir. There are dozens of labels in the English language for individuals who are a source of authority.

Throughout history we have celebrated these kings and queens because they bring order. Because autocrats almost always make laws that forbid their subjects from doing harm to neighbors we know where we stand and people live in peace.

It is clear that giving an individual absolute authority to make law is not a good idea.

→ Absolute power corrupts absolutely.

→ In the past, without exception individuals controlling absolute political power have justified giving themselves and their friends' privilege because they have might or a divine right from God.

→ When there is a group in society with privilege, by definition, it is essential to have a group who are underprivileged.

→ Privileged groups **oppress** underprivileged groups.

→ In your dictionary you will find the antonym of oppression is **liberty**.

→ **Liberty** can be defined as, the quality or state of being free. Rather than just another word for nothing left to lose, I like to think of liberty as freedom with ownership and responsibility.

→ Oppression brings out the worst in human beings just as liberty brings out the best.

→ When people are oppressed they don't smile much, they do horrible things to each other and they are not as honest. (Questionable assertion, you judge. I remember an interview of a Russian hockey player in the 1972 Canada-Russian series saying he noticed people in the west smiled and laughed more than in his home land.)

→ If you read history you will find the second most popular source of authority is monotheism or, simply, a single religion. In theory, the laws produced by using the authority of a God, the head of a belief system, who is omniscient and impartial, should be the best.

Western Europe experimented using a single belief system as a source of authority in the early part of the fourth century when Emperor Constantine converted to Christianity. Roman Catholicism became the source of authority in Western Europe following the collapse of the Western Roman Empire. Historians call this the medieval period. Some historians use the term the dark ages because of the incredible **oppression**. People did heinous things to each other under this oppression. You can find stories of people burning living women tied to stakes or stretching human bodies on a rack until the joints dislocate and then throwing the still living bodies, filled with incredible pain, into a dungeon to rot. Because the people were absolutely controlled by the church, in mind, body and spirit they took no ownership or responsibility in what the modern world would think of as crimes. Considering this period lasted for over a thousand years there was little technological or scientific progress.

People living in jurisdictions using monotheism (single religion) as a source of authority, in modern times, report oppression. The most popular modern monotheisms are Islamic states using the Koran and the Muslim belief system as their source of authority. Although the oppression is far less than the oppression found in the medieval period, where Roman Catholicism was used as a source of authority, it still causes factions which justify heinous acts. We have all heard stories of people strapping bombs to living young people, sending them into crowded places and then exploding the human bombs.

→ The third and least popular source of authority in our history is to use the mass of the people to democratically elect a government. In modern western societies we use our governments as our source of authority. Governments have one simple job. The citizens in democratic jurisdictions charge their government with the responsibility of making the most effective and efficient laws. Most western jurisdictions use a representative or participatory democracy.

→ Within our governments we have dominant philosophies like socialism, communism and capitalism. These isms are good in theory but in practice fail because of the inherent autocratic oppression generated by the granting of privilege to law makers. The complexity of modern politics comes from managing the age old practice of giving groups and individuals' privilege. Another word for privilege is monopoly. Monopoly is not a bad thing if there is a consensus of citizens solidly behind monopolistic law.

→ As I said earlier, people have never lived so well as we do in western society using representative governments elected by the mass of the people on a regular basis. Un-corrupted, elected governments produce an environment of liberty. People smile and laugh, they are more generous, creative, innovative, honest and they don't, generally, do horrible things to each other.

→ Liberty is good. Oppression should be avoided at all costs.

Chapter 3 *The Flaw*

→ There is however one small flaw in our representative democracy. The flaw is the question of legitimacy. Is there a solid consensus behind each law produced by our representative governments? Is there a consensus of citizens in a jurisdiction who agree with the law? In western democratic societies we don't know if there is a consensus. This ignorance is the flaw.

Now, after this short lesson, you as a good citizen, can judge laws from the perspective of interference, oppression and legitimacy. This is one of your responsibilities as a citizen. By using the three elements of law, from your perspective, you can question any given law.

→ Does the law minimize interference between people going about their (lives) business?

→ Does the law minimize oppression by eliminating privilege?

→ (And now the most important part of each law.)
Is the law legitimate? Is it known beyond any shadow of doubt that there is a solid consensus, a large number of interested citizens in a jurisdiction, who agree with the law?

Over a period of time, the ignorance of knowing or not if there is consensus, (the flaw) will weaken our governments. With each questionable law, the cost of administering and enforcing laws escalates. Maintaining bureaucracies, increasing security, overburdening judicial systems and building new jails to incarcerate non-conforming citizens is very expensive. As the costs mount and more citizens balk at questionable law the authority of governments deteriorate, allowing privilege to vested interest groups (corporate plutocracies) and ultimately revolutionary forces will weaken the authority of our elected governments.

Rome had a similar problem with their republic in the last century BC. Although the history is not without debate it seems for decades the Roman Republic had been in a state of political paralysis. In 44 BC the Roman Senate, in a desperate move, succumbed to autocratic rule. The first Emperor, Gaius Julius Caesar "dictator in perpetuity" became the source of authority displacing the authority of the Republic of Rome. It is said that Julius's rule only lasted nine months; however, before the Senators of Rome managed to kill him, Julius had managed to **create laws** making it impossible to get rid of the institution of Emperor. Augustus Caesar (Gaius Octavius, the adopted son of Julius Caesar) became the individual who took over as the source of authority after the death of Julius.

At this point I would like to make it quite clear; I do not advocate changing our governments in any way. Our governments have the ability to produce excellent, well thought out laws which should be honed through many checks and balances. I am not an advocate of changing our electoral system. Our electoral systems do a good job of putting warm bodies in the seats of our governments. I am an advocate of **changing the largest part of our democracy, the citizens. It is time people stop believing in Kings, Gods and Politicians and start believing in themselves and their fellow citizens.**

The citizen pays the highest price for this flaw of ignorance because it takes away their liberty. Citizens don't have ownership or responsibility for the laws made by our representative governments. As a people we suffer from this lack of liberty. Jean Jacque Rousseau, the French Revolution Philosopher, made the statement, "Man imposes his own freedom." When we impose ownership and responsibility on ourselves we produce freedom which equals liberty. In a representative democracy the ownership and responsibility is so diluted the citizens don't feel they have liberty.

When my children turned 16 they got drivers licenses. We were pleased to lend them our cars. They were responsible to a point but often would bring my or my wife's car, home with little or no gasoline, who knew if there was air in the tires, oil in the engine or if the car needed a wash. My son got a job and bought a car. I watched him wash, wax and vacuum his car. He checked the fluids, the tire pressure and even had his friends come over to lift the car so that he could check the brake linings. This is the change I expect when people realize they have ownership and responsibility in making law. Generally it is possible to pick out rental or social housing units when you drive down residential streets. People who have ownership and responsibility take more care. When people have ownership and responsibility in making law we can expect a dramatic shift for the betterment of our world.

Some of us lament the past where people were self-sufficient. Their very lives were dependent on their resourcefulness and creativity. They had ownership and responsibility filling them with a sense of freedom. In my childhood I watched families grow, can, and preserve food for winter. They were happy strong and resilient people with little reliance on grocery stores. Since then this ownership and responsibility has been diluted, diminishing our liberty, making our lives less meaningful and fostering the bad side of humanity. If anything, today we are moving towards a fortress mentality because we have ownership and responsibility inside our property but at the same time we ignore what is going on outside our residence.

When in public spaces our governments treat us like welfare cases. Public officials have good reason to mistrust modern citizens because they know citizens have no ownership or responsibility. Yellow clad police will not be necessary, at public gatherings to herd the masses, if citizens have ownership and responsibility. Not only are we missing the important social interactions of working together towards accomplishing goals but our decision makers are missing the accumulated wisdom of citizens when it comes to producing the most efficient and effective laws.

It is impossible to measure the financial cost of the flaw but think for a minute, about the escalating cost of security. Billions are spent on policing, software security, automobile security, building security and maintaining government secrecy. People who live in an environment of liberty are less likely to have reasons to lie, cheat or pillage.

Our society has propagated the idea of good people and bad people. Most of us, if given the chance to judge good and bad, would judge ourselves as trustworthy, good people. Where do the bad people come from? Babies are all good. People grow from babies. Somewhere between the infant stage and adulthood people morph into what society judges as good or bad. If we are all good we don't need to spend billions on security. Again the original argument about liberty and oppression can explain why western democratic societies are better. People are better when they live in an environment of liberty or freedom with ownership and responsibility. Notice the millions of enlightened people who are migrating (legally or not) to western democracies.

In a dictatorship it is the physical body of the citizen that is oppressed. In a communist regime the mind and the body are oppressed. In monotheism the body, the mind and spirit are oppressed. In a true democracy the body, the mind and the spirit are liberated, unmasking the good side of humanity.

Most of us spend a good part of our lives earning privilege through education, by growing a business or by lobbying government for special privilege within law. It is not hard to find people who think the laws, giving privilege to components of our society, are increasingly unfair. Commercializing our world causes economic oppression, a concept akin to slavery. Instead of using the best technology, citizens are forced to use inferior technology (why not have an operating system using the best of Microsoft and Apple) because the holders of privilege monopolize intellectual property. Oil companies, big box stores, big pharmaceutical companies, the arms industry and monopolistic agricultural companies earn privilege in law through lobby groups. Our representative governments protect this privilege producing economic oppression exposing the dark side of humanity.

If we can fix the flaw we can start moving toward a trusting society. The millions of laws our governments produce are like a tightening noose around our necks. Something beautiful is dying. This tightening noose is oppression. People don't smile as much as they should and they lie, cheat and steal more than they would in an environment of liberty. The individual is paying a huge price because our governments are not producing effective, economical and quality laws which are known to be legitimate. Instead I understand there are two laws on the books for each citizen in the USA. This amounts to almost a billion laws, and many are useless. Harvey Silverglate describe how we all, unknowingly brake laws every day in his book "Three Felonies A Day".

Everything seems so simple after it is done for the first time. The people living a hundred years from now will know how simple it is to fix our political problems. These people will look back at our society and wonder how could we have lived like we do? How could we afford the cost of an oppressive society? How could we carelessly allow our environment to be torn to pieces because of the avarice of a few? How could we stifle the innovation and creativity and, above all, how could we thoughtlessly take away the joy of life from our people?

Our political world has been shaped by the works of Niccolo Machiavelli who in 1531 wrote "The Prince". He observed, political success does not come from being a good guy but rather can only occur if one follows the example of the most devious politicians. Hard line politicians follow his ideas and with a cunning sociopathic intelligence, lacking remorse for those who suffer, accomplish their goals. If a politician says they know what the people want they are being dishonest. They know only what their supporters and friends want. Even the most advanced polls can be misleading. Politicians (because they believe they are somehow superior) who say they believe in democracy and at the same time insist they are doing the right thing, rather than bending to public opinion, are paternalistic and in fact dishonest. Although goals can be accomplished with this hard headed approach it should be noted that Machiavelli's Europe continued to be in turmoil and in some ways his books exacerbated unrest and violence for centuries after his death. Participative democracy produces a powerful legitimate authority eliminating the need for Machiavellianism which some feel is necessary to accomplish goals using a representative democracy.

Law makers have an obligation to the people to make laws which minimize interference between people going about their (lives) business, minimize oppression by eliminating aspects of privilege in the laws and insuring only laws where there is a known solid consensus are passed. Legitimate laws with consensus are economical, effective and free of oppression.

Chapter 4   *Consensus*

Consensus (Latin) -agreement, harmony, accord, unity, unanimity, solidarity.

I like the word consensus because it doesn't necessarily mean majority. In any given election the winner rarely has the backing of the majority of citizens. Many citizens are happy to be led. The important consideration is indoctrinating the fact, at an early age, that each citizen in a democratic society has ownership and controls exactly the same amount of political authority (POPA) from the age of consent until the end of life. With this understanding laws will be made, by citizens, to insure that each and every citizen, doesn't matter who they are, have equal access to controlling their POPA twenty-four seven, three hundred and sixty five days a year. The decision of participation is left to each citizen. This is defined as informed consent. By not acting the citizen is in fact participating by saying they are happy with the status quo.

Almost without exception when I use ancient Greece as an example of a participative democracy someone will stand up, usually a well-educated woman, and make the statement "women and slaves were not included, how can you call that a democracy?" This is a true and valid statement. Depending on which period in the Golden Age of Athens you are talking about only eight to twenty percent of the population controlled their POPA.

In ancient Attica if you went to a public space with say ten people there would be one or two who controlled political authority. However, in modern times, we can go to a gathering of twenty thousand people and there won't be a single person there who controls their POPA. E**ven though we call ourselves**

citizens, the common person is politically equivalent to a woman or a slave in Ancient Greece. This situation **was** acceptable before our society developed the technology to tally with absolute ease consensus; however it is completely unacceptable in today's technological world. Not only is it unacceptable to not tally consensus but it is also unacceptable to allow the economic playing field to become so skewed to favor those holding privilege within law that people have given up participating.

We all know, even if we achieve a participative democracy, only a small percentage will participate. This is acceptable because no one should be forced to participate. We (each individual) have been given our POPA upon the age of consent. We understand what it means and how it works through our public education system and will always have the discretion to do what we think best.

By using the percentage of consensus rather than majority we can make legitimate law through a process of informed consent.

He who is silent, when he ought to have spoken and was able to, is taken to agree. Latin proverb.

Chapter 5 *Authority*

Authority; Power, command, control, dominance, rule, expert, right, license:

This word from Roman law (Latin: auctoritatis), is often replaced with the word power or political power. Both attempt to bring human beings together to work towards a common end, however they differ in the question of legitimacy. The concept of authority is an indispensable characteristic of all living things.

Many societies use the father or the oldest male as the source of authority in the family. At the beginning of the twenty-first century, in Western Society, if the family is lucky enough to have a mother and father, authority is generally shared between husband and wife, with children heavily influencing decisions. Families that understand the difference between oppression and liberty give each member ownership and responsibility in family decisions. There is little tension when members work through problems, finding solutions in open and free debate with a consensus of members making the final decision. The responsibilities for unforeseen consequences are shared by the entire family and as a group the entire family will learn and share the outcome. I feel comfortable hanging around families who practice liberty.

Forever humanity has suffered from gender-bias. Men have used their physical strength to oppress women. In the past social constructs were designed around the sentiment of the gender-bias of male superiority. A hundred years ago many women in western society bravely fought for suffrage. They successfully obtained full citizenship and the right to vote.

The resulting positive change has transformed our world into a better place. However the backlash of well-earned anti-male sentiment has put pressure on the male side of our species diluting rather than enhancing the many gifts only men can give. Participative democracy has the power to break down the toxic inequalities between the sexes. **In a participative democracy there is no recognition of gender.** When each of us is politically equal we will be able to open our hearts and let our love flow freely towards our families and society in general.

Before suffrage the courts considered a man's home his castle. Before the year nineteen hundred and twenty there were no laws preventing spousal abuse or male tyranny. Of course there is a full spectrum of men just as there were kings. Some men were gentle and kind some not so much. Modern literature seems to dwell on excessive tyranny while ignoring the huge majority of men who in fact were wonderful examples of benevolence. When I was young the father had absolute authority in the home. Absolute power corrupts absolutely. There is a full spectrum of how people deal with absolute power. In some families I witnessed spousal abuse, husbands beating wives and abusing children. In others I was envious of the love, caring, trust and respect husband and wife had for each other. In my life time laws have been made in a painfully slow process to stop tyranny in the family. However these laws in many cases have proved to be divisive, ineffectual and unfair. In a participative democracy where each citizen knows they control equal political authority we may find these laws are unnecessary.

A person such as a medical doctor or anyone with a PhD from an accredited university has intellectual authority. High-ranking religious individuals have religious authority just as the leaders of environmental and human rights groups have moral authority (Greenpeace). In a democracy the only legitimate source of political authority in a jurisdiction is consensus from the mass of its people. **By definition, laws made using**

consensus are liberating not oppressive. Unfortunately, a representative democracy can only produce laws made with questionable authority. We respect these laws, even though they are not ours, because they give us a framework to live within, minimizing interference which is magnitudes better than no law. However, laws made with legitimate authority are better.

Nature is filled with order resulting from natural authority relying on an imposed co-operation between species. Naturally we think of authority as having power over another. Because of the nature of man, this authority over another usually means oppression.

When a right wing government is elected, the authority of the right wing government makes laws which oppress the left wing opposition and vise-versa. When we work under the authority of a boss, not because we want to but because we must pay your bills, we are oppressed. Organized labor oppresses employers balancing out work place oppression.

At a different level a dictator oppresses his citizens with fear and intimidation. In our modern world, with few exceptions, we are all oppressed. If we are the boss, the taxman, unions or the next level of authority oppress us.

Some corporations have recognized the improved effect of giving their employees autonomy in their work places by implementing modern participative management techniques. Unfortunately most of those companies do not have their headquarters in America, but rather Japan, or other new democracies where management change is still possible. It is easy to see how successful they are by looking at the brands of high tech equipment and automobiles on our roads.

Aristotle noted. "People want to be left alone to go about their lives without interference". The problem being, people going about their lives interfere with others. This is where politics come in. We need the authority of rules and regulations to minimize interference between people going about their business. If the laws are legitimate, made using a consensus of citizens, then they are by definition, free of oppression. Using consensus from the mass of the people to produce legitimate laws will minimize oppression and change citizens from inward looking critics to happy, joyful citizens with a sense of purpose.

To understand what influences the making of law, one must realize the spectrum of authority. I have chosen Cosmos, Bios, Demos, and Ethnos to describe the levels of this spectrum.

The Authority of the Cosmos;

(The COSMOS: an orderly or harmonious system) Pythagoras first used the word perhaps to describe the starry firmament of the sky. In this case we will use Cosmos in a spiritual way. Perhaps we can think of it as another dimension or a parallel universe. If we can't find the answer to a question, like what happens after we die, let's use the cosmos as a place to explain it.

Because human beings are cognitive we are able to use our imagination to create realities. All individuals in every society have imagined realities which often find their way into social constructs. Language, money, religions and the concept of corporations, are social constructs that don't exist but in our minds are rock solid.

The cosmos, this place that exists only in our minds, is the highest level of authority. This is where our ancestors speculated the Gods and the spiritual beings live controlling the Bios (nature). They controlled the wind, the rain; they brought plagues and built great empires. The cosmos is a place where the dead live on the other side of the river Styx. It's where the stars and the planets roamed until astronomers slowly removed them from the cosmos through research.

Many religions have divided the cosmos into heaven and hell. Heaven is where God and his son live. This is where the Buddhists go after they are enlightened (Nirvana). The Muslims go to Mohamed in paradise and mix with Allah. Deep inside every human there is a cosmos, a place to explain death. To the human soul nothing has more authority than death. If **someone holds a gun to your head they have the ultimate authority over you, the authority of the Cosmos.** Throughout history tyrants have used the authority of the cosmos to control people. The authority of our ancestors comes from the cosmos, and upon birth we are all given a ticket to return.

The Authority of the Bios
The AUTHORITY of the BIOS is not an imagined reality. It is the authority of all living things. It is spring flowers bursting open exposing their reproductive organs to probing insects. It is early morning red blood cells pulsing through the arteries of a jogger running down a city street. It is chloroplasts poised to move with the gentle light of sunrise on a cool spring morning. And it's birds shouting out their song of love in the early morning dampness. We call it the balance of nature, the struggle for survival. Placed before us undisturbed by man this balance exceeds our understanding of order. To understand the power of the Bios consider the love between a man and women and the authorities people will trample to fulfill their love. Shakespeare described this authority in his play Romeo and Juliet where two young lovers defy the authority of their tribes to be together. Consider the drive to survive, to eat, to reproduce. Compare the mating behavior of humans to other animals; the joy we get from dressing up and adorning ourselves with beautiful cloths and make up; how we love to go to parties and flaunt our beauty. All these activities are part of the authority of the Bios.

All species including man are under enormous genetic pressure (the authority of the bios) from our ancestors. Throughout our lives, without knowing why, we change. Our bodies change, our thought processes change and we do things that a decade earlier would be personally unacceptable. Because of genetic diversity each individual fits into a different part of the spectrum of our species. Successful traits found in each individual, be they judged good or bad, make each of us unique.

Before civilizations, our tribal ancestors existed inside the authority of the Bios. They were hunters and gatherers, with no central authority. The Bios is the interface between the Cosmos and life, birth into the bios, death into the cosmos. It is also a giant experimental lab, a place filled with natural and sexual selection giving credence to Darwin's ideas of diversity and survival of the fittest.

Environmental groups like Greenpeace use the authority of the Bios to justify interfering with commercial activities. The ancestors of people who populate our planet today evolved in the womb of the Bios. As said earlier each of us is under enormous pressure from our ancestors (nature) to reproduce and carry on our successful family. Without nature, man and his authority cannot exist.

The Authority of the Demos

The DEMOS is a concept of authority, which comes from people joining together to form a central authority. The key words are **people make an authority**. The authority of the demos has been formed from many imagined realities which form social constructs (laws). The common ingredient in all civilizations and societies is a central authority (social construct). Without authority we have anarchy and move back into the authority of the Bios. This option appeals to some political thinkers who consider themselves anarchists and like the idea of using the Bios as their source of authority.

Authority motivates people into co-operation. From this perspective, all civilizations have something in common. They have a central authority. The difference between civilizations is the source of their authority. The Chinese Empire, the most enduring civilization, which spans some 5,000 years, has almost exclusively used an individual or ruler as a source of authority. Western Society has used a variety of individuals with a plethora of names like King, Queen, Emperor etc..

The second most popular source of authority in the Demos is a theocracy (one religion or specifically monotheism). The rulers in these jurisdictions use the authority of the cosmos (God). In our modern day it's not difficult to find a society utilizing a belief system as a source of authority. As said earlier Muslim countries utilize the Koran; some orthodox Christians use the bible. Historians tell us western civilization used the Catholic belief system as a source of authority from the time of Constantine in the fourth century AD, until the Renaissance in the twelfth century.

The least common source of authority is democracy, or using the Demos or mass of the people as a source of authority to make law. In a true democracy laws are made with consensus. We impose our laws on ourselves thus creating an environment of liberty. Using people as a source of authority is the most complicated. It is a relatively new concept beginning in antiquity with what we know of as a Greek City State. Historians tell us Athens and Rome both began as Greek City States; Rome moved towards a representative participatory democracy with their republic while Attica (ancient Greece) used participative democracy. Although using people (democracy) as a source of authority has been rarely used in our history, it has proved to attract people who want to improve the quality of their lives as evidenced in the mass migration of desperate people from countries where there is little or no liberty.

Switzerland used direct democracy at the end of the 14th century, hundreds of years before the Americans' built their republic. The British and her commonwealth countries reluctantly gave the common citizen an opportunity to participate early in the 20th century. If the per-capita income of countries having early democracies is any indication of their success, then all nations should be working to increase the democratic aspects of their governments.

Most Western nations use some form of representative democracy (participatory democracy) where citizens are given an opportunity on a regular basis to participate in the question of who will use citizens' authority to make law for their jurisdiction.

Authority is a word commonly used in our modern world as a person or group of people (Committee) responsible for making decisions; examples are Health Authority, Education Authority, and Transportation Authority. The concept is entirely man made thus the source of authority comes from the Demos.

Governments and Industry operate using these extremely complicated mechanisms of Annual Conventions, Boards, committees and subcommittees filled with rules of order and parliamentary procedures. This subletting of authority works but some believe it to be inefficient, self-serving, and fraught with disillusioned participants and sometimes-angry people that must suffer decisions favoring those with authority.

Citizens' initiatives like plebiscites, referendums, and recall processes are crude forms of direct democracy, however there is no engineering in the process and the results are often contradictory, ineffectual and a waste of time. Brexit is an example of poorly engineered direct democracy that has failed.

Despite the criticisms, people living in Western Society have never lived better. With the exception of arms technology, even nations using an individual or belief system benefit from the spin offs of western society.

The Authority of the Ethnos

Inside every society there is a brewing **Ethnos**. This is the most destructive level of authority. It can utilize a ruler, a belief system, or people as its source of authority. The Ethnos works from within an established jurisdiction, but outside the established political authority. A common part of the Ethnos is the savage underground economy of drugs, prostitution, gang warfare, smuggling and political subterfuge. Any normal human activity deemed illegal by the official government will without exception become part of the Ethnos. Laws, made with questionable authority, interfering with normal human activity, should be considered an incentive to crime.

Oppression of underprivileged people inside a jurisdiction will cause dangerous anti-establishment groups. There have been cases where religious groups have replaced the established authority with the authority of a belief system. (Persia to Iran) Often there is a vested interest in the formation of factions in society responding to some inequality. Usually the Ethnos responds in kind plus some (civil disturbance) and may become powerful enough to over-throw the existing authority.

Human beings love watching the murder and carnage in civil disturbances as evidenced by the popularity of movies and documentaries made using civil disturbance as their subject matter. A few examples of ethnos taking over an established authority are, the French Revolution, Ireland, the American war of Independence and Civil War, the Serbs and the Croatians of Yugoslavia and the Hutus and the Tootsies of Uganda.

Ancient history is a chronicle of endless war among jurisdictions and civil disturbances within. There is one anomaly. Before democracy the Plains of Attica (ancient Greece) were alive with ethnos and continuing civil disturbance. This changed after the democratic principles of the citizen's assembly became the highest authority in the land with the proclamation, by Cleisthenes in 508 BC. The laws made by the accumulated authority of the Citizens' Assembly were final. The noted historian Sir Moses Finley tells us that after the democratic reforms in 508 BC there was a lack of civil disturbance inside Attica for some 300 years. The foundation for Western Civilization was nurtured in this fertile environment.

There is little threat of revolution or political upheaval caused by the ethnos (anti-government factions) in most modern democracies because it is difficult to make laws that blatantly reduce the quality of life of the bulk of citizens. However because no one knows if laws made by representative governments are legitimate, (a consensus of citizens are in favor of the outcome) anyone can oppose the law and build a larger ethnos. The cost of controlling the ethnos escalates as our communities move away from democratic political systems.

Chapter 6

Motivation

Motivation; The reasons one has for acting or behaving in a particular way. Incentive, stimulus, inspiration, or the general desire or willingness to do something; to stop hunger, to fulfill spirituality, to build a family, to find external reward (money), or the pursuit of art, science or truth.

All creatures either live to reproduce or reproduce to live. The act of leaving self-replicating DNA in an environment where it will be able to reproduce is the motivation for the essence of life. Our biosphere is filled with the magic of reproduction. There are good arguments to say that all the incentives, we have as a species, are connected to our need to reproduce and survive. For a billion years the essence has been diversity. Each surviving species has had enough diversity to survive environmental changes up until the present. The human genus has survived a competitive struggle not only with competing species but also within our own species.

There are many reasons people do things. They act because of love, status, hunger, fear, to fulfill a dream, to survive, because of guilt, patriotism, to find a place where they can be free or because they love gardening. It is possible to see a full spectrum of interesting traits, from the extreme obsession to wash continually (obsessive compulsive disorder) to people who are continually looking at themselves in the mirror and are willing to spend the majority of their disposable income on maintaining and enhancing their image.

Abraham Maslow published "A Theory of Human Motivation," in 1943 based on a pyramid of human needs. The foundation of the pyramid is comprised of food, water, air, security, law, order and stability. The next level is our need for love and belonging followed by the third layer of our need to grow and achieve recognition for our improved skills and accomplishments. Finally at the top of the pyramid is self-actualization. At this level an individual is content knowing they have done their best, have accomplished many things in their life, and that they are loved and can now live as they please in a world of liberty without fear or oppression.

Since Maslow, there have been libraries of books written on human motivation. There are armies of social engineers who have used these theories to motivate people in our free market to go into debt to purchase goods and services in order to make the captains of our society wealthy. In so many ways our motivation has become singular. The sentiment that money is the solution to all problems is a fundamental belief in our societies. Money fulfills the needs of the first layer of Maslow's pyramid and can help with the third but its effect on love, belonging, and skill are secondary and often blunt attempts to achieve self-actualization.

Companies and corporations are instruments created by the legal systems in our societies. The reality is, like money they are legal fictions. They only exist in our minds. They provide individuals, with common interests, rules and regulations within a group.

Individuals use the concept of incorporation to limit their personal liability from their working life as a professional. Incorporation takes away the responsibility an unincorporated individual would normally carry. The legal instrument of corporation treats the corporation as an individual without the right to vote. However inside our representative democracies corporations have lobbying powers and the wealth to use social engineering to influence real change between elections. One might see the individual as having privilege over a corporation because they can vote, however, in a representative democracy the citizen has no control over their POPA between elections.

This is a key point. In a participative democracy the political landscape changes allowing citizens to compete with corporations between elections because the citizen controls their POPA twenty-four hours a day, three hundred and sixty-five days a year.

Incorporated volunteer organizations and charity groups are often motivated solely to fulfill a need in society. However the vast majority of corporations are motivated by money and the need for power to make more money by controlling the economic environments they exist in. Although they can't vote for a representative in government, corporations use lobby groups to obtain influence in government to make laws giving them privilege.

The argument **for** Corporations is they supply almost all the wonderful products we use. Because of this man made instrument, created by our democratic societies, our quality of life has increased. In some ways corporations have joined the world together by producing, at very little cost, sophisticated equipment to allow the world to communicate. Because corporations can span political borders they have spread ideas and culture. Coca-Cola, McDonald's, Samsung, Toyota, and Ford can be found almost everywhere irrespective of political borders.

The economy of scale is a common argument in support of the corporate model. However, producing goods and services en-mass takes away the individual's need to be self-sufficient. We are losing ownership and responsibility in our lives. Our motivation to achieve recognition is diminished. At this time in history corporations have served us well. The question: is there danger in the corporate model and is it possible to achieve even greater success using corporate models that are motivated only by the interests of the mass of our citizens? (Socialism in a participative democracy?).

Maslow's pyramid is a good model to describe what motivates us. The quality of our lives on the first layer, in some ways, has been over supplied, causing medical problems resulting from overeating and lack of exercise. Because large numbers of people in Western Society are dependent on this overabundance there is no foundation to build the top three layers of Maslow's pyramid. To find meaning in life we have an unending supply of popular self-help programs and books that profess to help people. In so many ways this is like trying to build a house without a foundation.

I often ponder the question: have the corporations that supply us with cheap goods and services made us so dependent that we have lost our confidence in our place on this planet? Have our representative democracies built this legal instrument not knowing they have removed the essence of our lives and made it impossible to achieve self-actualization?

On the other side of the coin there are people who put themselves in situations where they must provide for themselves to survive in the absence of our corporate overlords. Adventurous people, who climb mountains, walk for hundreds of miles with nothing but the clothes they wear and live in questionable situations in the hearts of cities, are searching for meaning. I have been part of a group (the cruising community) where people sail small boats to sparsely inhabited lands where it is essential to be self-sufficient. Although this life is difficult the people seem happy. I have noted in this group an abundance of creative innovation, generosity, love, a sense of well-being and an absence of prejudice. It seems easy for these people to climb through the layers of Maslow's pyramid and I know many of my sailing acquaintances have reached and gone beyond self-actualization.

The majority of companies use a mono-incentive model to fulfill their mission. They have only one incentive, "**money**". Such a mono-incentive is an unhealthy situation, a vile word, akin to monotheism, to describe the incredible oppression they are capable of. These monitory corpuses are capable of eroding the authority of our democratic societies and making law based on the single motivating force of money. The probable result is a stratified society where a very few will control all. Power and wealth will prevail with the justification of meritocracy and divine right. There are many examples where profits have dried up and the titans of industry have taken their wealth into gated communities while the people that made them wealthy struggle to survive.

As long as economies produce profits for hungry corporations citizens will get good quality products and services at a good price while employed people will reap the rewards of their labor. It is called the economy of scale. There is no problem with a corporation that is controlled by citizens, but when mono-incentive corporations control our governments we are in trouble. Increasingly, corporate lobby groups and armies of social engineers are manipulating law in order to give themselves privilege which translates into more profits. Many studies show that wealth is increasingly being focused on fewer and fewer individuals.

This is where participative democracy will shine. When each individual citizen and each individual corporation knows they have political equality with ownership and responsibility, a new wave of **motivation** with creativity based on common sense and co-operation will slowly build a new world. If there is a better way of producing goods and services, corporations had better sharpen their pencils and do a better job or they will become extinct. The only possible outcome in a participative democracy is a level playing field in an absence of hubris. Just like the unincorporated citizens, corporations will be driven by many incentives. Decreasing profits to gain status and improve the quality of goods and services will be as important as the money they make. There is a probability that we will see deflation as companies struggle to produce the best long lasting products. When this happens we can all take more time off and enjoy life.

Chapter 7

The Free Market Economy Compared to Representative Government.

I know it is counter-intuitive to believe that when each citizen controls equal political authority our societies will be more ordered, our governments will be more effective and they will have more authority to make effective change. The aristocracy of the eighteenth century argued that a free market economy would fail and drive Europe into chaos. A good argument for a participative democracy is the success of our free market economy.

Before Adam Smith, no one knew what a free market economy was. Aristocrats controlled our economies. Adam Smith advocated a free market giving every participant, the buyers and the sellers, **equal opportunity** to produce, purchase and market goods and services. His book "An Inquiry into the Nature and cause of the Wealth of Nations" was published in 1773.

In our recent history we have good examples of both controlled and free economies. The Soviet Union boasted about how they had organizations to control the production and distribution of goods for their people. The Soviet Government until 1989 denied their citizens equal opportunity in the marketplace. They talked about how stable their economy was compared to the out-of-control free market economy of the West. The differences between the two are enormous and although there are many problems with the free market economy it appears to improve the quality of life of the entire spectrum of society.

Our western marketplace is controlled by participants, not government. Because of this we are able to walk into any shop and find the best selection, price and quality of goods and services. In our western societies we have economists who, like our political scientists, analyze our economies and construct principles of good economic practice. In order to maintain honesty our economies have accountants who are the backbone of our free market economy. Why don't we have political engineers, the equivalent of accountants, in our economic system?

I would like to equate the communist economic system to our present political system. Both systems control, from the top down, citizens with absolute authority. Both systems allow very little input from the people and do not use the individual as a resource. The free market economy is a wonderful example of a participative democracy. We all participate by "voting with our dollar". People control what is on store shelves by selecting the best quality, the best price and in some cases where and who made the products.

Old communist jurisdictions used a *controlled economy.* Soviet professionals, who apparently had huge amounts of information at their fingertips, controlled production and distribution of goods for their people. (I learned this directly in Morse code on my ham radio and was almost convinced.) Western societies use a controlled political system. (representative democracy). Logically the controlled communist economic system should work better than the uncontrolled free market economy, just as a representative democracy should work better than a participative democracy. However, it's quite obvious that the opposite is true, at least when it comes to economics.

A participative democracy will improve politics just as our free market economy has improved our lives in contrast to what it was like to live in a Soviet controlled economy.

Almost all the surviving communist countries have captured the strength of the free market economy by handing over control of the market to their people. In the last three decades China's economy has moved from subsistence to a powerful economy. There are many reasons for this change, but the most important is the change from a controlled economy to a form of communist free market economy.

Russia has become a democracy that gives privilege and monopolies to influential people. Their attempt to move towards a free market economy, where every person has equal opportunity, has been plagued by uncontrollable elites. These plutocrats have stifled the initiative of the individual in the same manner that our political system stifles the political initiative of potential leaders in a representative political system. A participative democracy will capture the collective wisdom of our citizens with an unlimited number of effective leaders not just a few representatives who for the most part are angry older males (often wealthy) who represent a narrow ideology.

The biggest barrier to political progress mankind is facing is how to indoctrinate its citizens with the fundamental principles of participative democracy. Instead of believing, as we do today, that the citizen controls little or no political authority, and only people like Justin Trudeau and Donald Trump have this privilege, in a participative democracy **each citizen**, including the most powerful leaders, control exactly the same amount of political authority. In the past people living in communist countries were indoctrinated to live with a controlled economy. They had no experience living in a free market economy. This ignorance made Soviets suspicious and distrusting of western economics just as citizens in western society are suspicious and distrusting of participative democracy.

No one on the planet today has the experience of living in a society where each citizen controls the same amount of political authority from the age of consent to the end of life. No one today has lived in a world where the biggest source of authority is female. I'm confident that if the people of the world have the experience of living in a free political system, they will never want to go back to our present antiquated system. The citizens of the future will, no doubt, consider or describe our present political system as barely adequate, just as we now know the communist economic system doesn't work as well as a free market economy.

Before we move away from our representative democracy it is absolutely essential we follow the historical example left to us by Solon when he set up a dual system of government in Attica (ancient Greece) in 600 BC. The citizen's assembly, for a period of some ninety years, had no political authority until the people had time to practice, perfect and achieve confidence in the participative system. In 508 BC   Cleisthenes's proclamation legitimized the Citizens' Assembly as the source of authority in Attica.

If one examines the good things about Western Societies, one notices a wonderful variety of affordable goods of excellent quality. This is because each economic citizen has equal opportunity to participate by competing to sell or voting on what they think is good and well-priced by buying it. This tradition is being eroded because our governments are increasingly making laws that give international corporations privilege. In the future citizens in a participative economy will insure that producers of goods and services enter into a competitive struggle with other producers. In a free market economy the survival and incentive for producers to make the best goods and provide the best services depends on choices made by economic citizens. When this incentive is taken away the quality of goods and services decline. Products have become increasingly cheap to buy but in the long term expensive because they have such short life spans. Representative democracy is powerless to cure this malady which is resulting in uncontrolled expansion of our land-fills.

Do our representative governments have the will and the authority to maintain a free market economy? Is our functioning economy at risk from giant banks like Goldman Sachs, monopolies, internet market places and big box stores?

Chapter 8   *Political Questions*

Living in a western civilization we can smugly look out the windows of our homes and marvel at a world filled with social justice, peace, security, an overabundance of goods and, hopefully, joy. How did we get here, and like the wealthy losing their wealth, should we worry about losing all these wonders?

Our addiction to injecting hydrocarbons into the arteries of our civilization is long past any chance of an easy withdrawal. Our collective consciousness knows it's wrong but is unable to create effective change. There is overwhelming evidence in our recorded history to support the notion that politics plays the largest role in supporting and maintaining the quality of our lives. Why, in our modern western democracies, does our collective conscience play such a small part in the decisions made by our political system? Is there a way to increase the political participation of our citizens without disrupting the fine political balance we've achieved in the western world?

Unfortunately representative (participatory) democracy in western society is old, cumbersome and ineffectual. Representative democracy does not have the authority to make the changes necessary to bring our world into equilibrium. It seems everyone knows we have serious problems needing urgent repairs but all we get from our political system is weak and ineffective laws. Experience tells us it doesn't matter who you elect; the result will be more of the same bad news and increasing taxes.

This writing is not about parliamentary reform, electoral reform or reforming our institutions. This writing is about political franchise or suffrage that will change **the most powerful part of our democracy, "the citizens".**

There are many what-if scenarios and this is one of them. Imagine if the people who live in western democracies demanded suffrage like their ancestors in the early part of the twentieth century? Ralph Nader, In his book, 'Only the Super Rich can Save us', asks the question 'what if the super-rich financed reform, fixing the government, returning power to the people, galvanized a movement for alternative forms of energy and advancing clean elections?' I applaud Ralph Nader's book. It gives me hope and I want to add one unlikely but very resilient aspect to this solution. We can fix the problems but we all must be a part of the solution, not just the super-rich.

Suffrage: The right to vote or run for office in public, political elections.

Future suffrage: Every citizen's right to participate in the making of laws with equal authority.

After the first great war of the twentieth century the landless soldiers of the British Empire returned with the argument that if they were good enough to die for the King they should be good enough to vote for a political representative. These disfranchised men, returning from the war were given the vote. The women of America and England, who had been fighting for political franchise for decades in the suffragette movement, were granted the right to vote for a representative soon after. We have a better world today because our ancestors had the courage to stand up to the authorities and demand their rights.

It is time to take up the call for a new suffrage. This time we will fight for the **political equality** of each and every human being, our individual political franchise, our **equal say in the laws made by our governments** and the future of our children. **Political equality** is worth fighting for. If we win there will be an absence of war, our economies will stabilize, the threat of overpopulation will end, we will be able to stop the destruction of our environment and our improved social structure will allow us to live happy fulfilling lives free of loneliness, fear and oppression.

Any change in our political system should be expected to take generations as it can only be accomplished through the population's acceptance of the new set of values and understandings. To rush into any political change would not only harm future potential growth, but could also destabilize our present system which is filled with checks and balances that work. On the other hand if we can't find support for the needed democratic change and if we wait too long we'll be lost in another totalitarian society run by the very wealthy who are increasingly using social engineering tools (advertising) to control the population. ***The most important thing is to begin.*** The citizens of Ancient Greece practiced using participative democracy for some ninety years before the authority of citizens was used to make law. People living today need time to do a proper well thought out job of reforming our law-making mechanisms.

Numerous excellent documentaries point out what will happen to our biosphere and society if we don't change course. These documentaries bring awareness to the issues and should stimulate the citizens of the world into open and free debate necessary to establish their validity and to plan a resolution to the upcoming crisis.

It's all very well to be informed about a problem but, in today's world, being informed is a useless exercise because **we have the equivalent control over our political authority as the women and slaves of ancient Greece.** Citizens in nations with representative democracies have become whiners' complainers and finger pointers taking no responsibilities for the unforeseen consequences of government decisions.

This writing offers a possible solution to this problem. By empowering the individual with full citizenship, responsibility, and ownership in these problems we will make laws with powerful legitimate authority not just wishy-washy accords.

Perhaps you have read books, watched documentaries or attended enough lectures about our ancestors, to get a tiny understanding of what it would be like to live in a world where there is no law against murder, rape or genocide. People living in the bosom of democratic western societies find it hard to understand that humanity has the potential to be the most dangerous, cunning and cruel creature on the planet. We worry about the killing power of the shark but the real threat is human beings in the wrong political environment. Some say we are nature's knives, put here to reduce the number of species on the planet. Not only are we the most dangerous predator on the planet, we're also the principle predator of our own species. Some believe our very success has come from this complicated survival strategy of killing by war and war rape to select out the most intelligent and beautiful to reproduce. It's quite natural for the soldiers of Serbia to murder the men of a village and then lock up the women to be used as sex slaves. All the great warriors of the past did similar things; the Ottomans, Genghis Khan, and almost all of our modern warriors. The best incentive to fight hard was the free sex at the end of the battle.

The Geneva Convention recognizes rape and sexual slavery as crimes against humanity but in the recent past these practices were not considered crimes but instead were encouraged to stimulate the troops and undermine the moral of the enemy. Today western society has **laws** preventing these crimes. We the people, who now live in an environment of liberty provided by western society, are not only the descendants of thousands of generations of people who survived genocide, murder and rape, but are also the people responsible for maintaining these laws preventing crimes against humanity.

Is the answer to the political question universal political equality and will this insure an absence of oppression and tyranny that was so prevalent in our past?

Chapter 9

The Big Picture

There is good evidence to support the notion that over the last billion years successive waves of life have populated the biosphere of earth. Scientists tell us the amount of carbon dioxide in the atmosphere decreased over a period of six hundred million years from twenty percent, when there was no life a billion years ago, to a value of around three hundred and fifty parts per million. Nitrogen and trace gases did not change. With the advent of life the amount of oxygen increased from almost nothing to around twenty percent. Scientists tell us this change occurred because of the organic process of photosynthesis and has been quite stable for the last four hundred million years. Life, as we know it, has adapted to the present oxygen and carbon dioxide levels. The biosphere is a very thin and fragile layer in relation to the size of the planet.

Can you imagine standing beside the planet earth looking at the surface? You would not be able to detect mountains. The world would be glassy smooth with a thin blue oxygen containing atmosphere. If you tried to touch the surface, the devastation on earth would probably not heal for thousands of years, not to mention you'd probably burn your finger as you entered the outer atmosphere. If you pushed hard on the surface you'd realize the earth's crust is as thick as the wall of a water balloon, filled with liquid magma with an iron pith.

Between the outer crust and the stratosphere there is a layer eight kilometers thick, at its thickest, where all the living creatures on earth live. It's so thin you would need a high-powered microscope to see it.

If you were an extraterrestrial being looking down, you might notice some unusual discoloration around London, New

York or Tokyo, but for the most part you'd only see ocean, land and cloud. After viewing the planet with a powerful microscope you might come to the realization that the slug like creatures that move along the roads are the machines of an even smaller creature, a species of primate that on closer inspection dominate the entire planet.

These primates seem to have unending vigor to grind up the surface of the planet using energy they derive by digging up ancient carbon deposits and burning them in their machines. If you studied the planet for long enough you'd realize this transformation was very unusual, and because it was happening at an ever-increasing rate some sort of outcome to bring the planet back to equilibrium must happen in the near future. How exciting to be the extraterrestrial scientist who just happened to be studying this planet at the perfect time to witness this change.

Perhaps you would stay and try to ascertain exactly what was happening. Maybe there are some records from previous visits to this planet giving you a clue to how this amazing evolutionary process had occurred. In the span of a little over a million years these primates have evolved from a small in number species fitting into a tiny niche in the environment with many closely related taxonomic groups to a species with a brain twice the size of their ancestors and no close species relatives.

When it comes to trying to grasp the amount of time the planet has existed, relative to the life time of a human, you might just as well give up. The human genus has existed for perhaps one point two million years and if we consider one generation being twenty years, then you have sixty thousand generations of ancestors. How much do you know about the last three generations of your own family? How much do we really know about the last three thousand years of recorded history? How much do we know about this speck of dust we call home relative to the mass of our galaxy or the tiny spec our galaxy is relative to the universe? Yes this thin layer, on this obscure planet, this biosphere, is where we evolved, where we live, and where we will always live.

This is our place. From outer space a storm can be seen traveling across the surface of the planet at a snail's pace, The fastest animals, birds, take a year to migrate over half of the planet. Some believe the first people to occupy the Americas took a thousand years to migrate from Alaska to Southern Chile.

Our biosphere has proved to be very durable. Life has survived cataclysmic asteroid events, periods of glaciation and volcanic winter. Our planet has never experienced a species that has the ability to end all life with nuclear explosions or upset some unforeseen balance. We are living in the blink of an eye and the question is; do we have the intelligence to grasp the big picture and maintain this paradise, this thin biosphere, on this tiny planet?

It's difficult, if not impossible, to rise above our lifetime of indoctrination, our prejudices and our religious beliefs. These beliefs are so embedded in some people that they find it reasonable to exploit our paradise even though their actions could inadvertently make our biosphere unlivable. Is there some way to control this out of control primate, the most dangerous, cunning and lethal creature to ever occupy this precious biosphere of this tiny planet? In my mind there's only one small possibility;

--politics.-

Chapter 10   *Moving Away From the Flat Political Earth Theory*

Most of us, at the thought of politics, unlike shopping, feel quite ill, a kind of nausea, where we feel oppressed and hopeless. Something we would rather ignore, if at all possible.

How would you like to live in a world where you hold politics as the dearest thing in your life, an institution you cherish, an institution that connects you to a world you love, a world where you have ownership, a place, and responsibility? Can you imagine politicians as your dearest friends? These leaders are your political equals controlling exactly the same amount of political authority as you. You know you can trust them to work for the betterment of all. Imagine loving politics as much as you love shopping.

It seems the average citizen of today has a different opinion. I've heard politicians described as untrustworthy scumbag exploiters of the common man. That the governments they participate in are shrouded in secrecy to protect their dishonesty. The sentiment is that to be a politician one needs a thick skin. Unfortunately, many politicians are also thick headed and not particularly intelligent people. They seem to be unaware of the consequences of the laws they are making. Laws that unknowingly lower the quality of life of the average citizen while compromising the future life on this planet. Do you believe that many of the laws made by politicians are made to satisfy their lust for power and wealth? Do you find elections are a **dog and pony show**, filled with spin and sentiment, rather than a process to select good people to rule? The traits needed to be a politician in today's world leave little room for intelligence. It is hard to find a politician who is as intelligent as your neighbor. One politician I personally know, when I asked why he was stepping down, whispered, "I can't associate with those morons." Politicians with any intelligence often step down rather than associate with people who have the correct traits to tolerate modern western politics.

Few read the writings of modern political scientists or political philosophers, probably because their dissertations shed no new light on pressing political problems. It is the same old boring stuff describing in detail the questionable corruption and stupidity of politicians who have notoriety. If you do read them I think you'll find these intellectuals almost exclusively write from the tangible, or realist perspective, carefully referencing their earlier works. All the wonderful ideas from the past are buried in the propaganda generated by the prejudices and fears of the great warlord heroes we read about in our history books.

Political Scientists are very good historians. They are good at accounting for and speculating on the outcomes in political competitions, but when it comes to finding answers to improving our political system, they leave that to the radicals and the revolutionaries. If we were talking about any other branch of science we would find engineers or accountants who come up with new ideas, new ways of doing things, and new technologies based on fundamental principles generated by scientists. Imagine if we only had physicists and mathematicians but no engineers to design and build our roads and bridges. An engineer knows how much steel and concrete is needed to build the center span of a bridge. They know how to efficiently move traffic. Physicists and mathematicians on the other hand don't have a clue about building bridges or roads. Political scientists know nothing about building a democratic political system but in both cases the foundation of understanding comes from the scientists. In political science there is a noticeable absence of engineers.

Imagine what our free market economy would be like if we only had economists and no accountants. If we used 200-year-old roads and bridges traffic would move slowly, it wouldn't be efficient and it would probably collapse under the weight of our modern world. Is this not what's happening with our hopelessly out of date representative democracies?

The last real change in the way laws are made in western democracies happened a few hundred years ago in the USA. Why are we so afraid to change our political system? Wouldn't it be ideal if we had political engineers to build roads and bridges of communication, giving the intelligence and common sense of the silent majority a role in decision-making? In a participative democracy political engineers will build mechanisms to smoothly bring forward the best solutions to needs or problems in our communities, in a process of moving towards consensus.

Do you feel you participate in the shaping of the laws your government makes? Do you hear your fellow citizens criticizing and complaining about government decisions, always using the expression "they should do this" or "they should do that"?

We (I will always try to use the word, "we" not "they") can change our politics, always moving towards sustainability in our environment, our social structure and our economy.

To understand the change I am talking about I would like to compare what we think of politics today to the understanding of our surroundings a thousand years ago.

Compare your beliefs in politics to the understanding of astronomy in the eleventh century. There was a belief that the earth was flat, resting on the back of a giant turtle and if you sailed too far off shore you would fall off. In modern politics we think our political authority ends at our border and citizens revolve around politicians. In a global participative democracy this dynamic changes; politicians revolve around citizens on a round political earth where each planetary citizen is responsible for the same amount of political authority.

Chapter 11

The Nature of Man

People in our modern world are under enormous genetic pressure to be like the sixty thousand generations of their ancestors. If we understand where these pressures come from we may be able to capture the beautiful side of humanity and suppress the destructive side.

Why do individuals with wealth, but no political authority build fortresses around themselves, become reclusive and think the rest of the world is somehow inferior? Why do individuals with too much political authority become tyrants, feel superior, treat people with disrespect and use their authority to benefit themselves while disrespecting the interests of the masses?

We need citizens who want to get involved, who feel ownership and have a responsibility for the well-being of our planet. If a citizen feels they have equal political authority they will get involved, they will feel ownership and responsibility for the planet and they will take on the responsibility for the future by working with other citizens to find legitimate law which will bring the planet to sustainability.

At the beginning of the twenty-first century man-made entities called "corporations" are competing with representative democracies to be the source of authority, eroding away the authority of our elected politicians. A blatant example was the 2008 corporate bailout. "Give us money and economic control over your people or the world will go into economic crisis." History is full of examples where the costs of bureaucracies exceed the ability of citizens to pay the taxes needed to maintain them. Governments are going into receivership and piece by piece are being bought out by eager corporations. The authority of the citizen's democracy is slowly vanishing in western society.

One way or another, the authority of our elected governments will diminish, just as the authority of the aristocracy in Western Europe diminished in the nineteenth century. If the citizens of our western democracies sit like frogs in a pot of warming water and do not recognize their peril, our descendants, at the end of the twenty-first century could be living in a total corporate tyranny worse than anything we know of today. On the other hand if there are enough of us who understand the benefits of participative democracy, there is a good chance our descendants will control corporations and use their beneficial aspects to build a world of liberty, peace and prosperity.

This is where we should think hard about what we really want. The number of science fiction books and movies predicting an oppressive future far outnumber those predicting peace and prosperity. Do we want our great great grandchildren to endure lives of unending oppression or should we begin a process of building a foundation for a sustainable future of peace and prosperity.

Humankind is unique in the animal world because we have imagination, (cognitive ability) which probably separates us from our animal cousins. Most of us have conscious, rational minds, but a few members of our species lack these attributes and find themselves on the end of the spectrum where they are known as sociopaths or in extreme cases psychopaths. Politics attracts people on this end of the spectrum justifying their actions with Machiavellian theory (It is easier to accomplish goals if you have no soul).

There have been many theories to answer the question; where did our intelligence come from in such a short period of time and why did Neanderthals and Denisovans disappear some twenty thousand years ago leaving Sapiens as the only surviving Hominin group .

Some believe a supreme being gave us our intelligence, as stated in the bible, "In seven days God created heaven and earth and made man in his image." The aristocracy of Western Europe used the concept they call **divine right from God** to justify their superior position over their people. Others believe space aliens genetically engineered us as demonstrated by the evidence uncovered in Von Daniken's documentary Chariots of the Gods and illustrated in the movie 2001 a Space Odyssey.

The Occam's Razor philosophy says the simplest explanation is probably correct. No one wants to think of their ancestors as brutes driven by their sex drive. It is easier to believe we are the children of God or the results of alien DNA. However, from reading recorded history and assuming the nature of man hasn't changed much in the last million years of prerecorded history the simplest answer is obvious.

Sexual selection gives a species enough genetic diversity to withstand environmental changes. When there is little environmental change species tend to put pressure on themselves. Brilliant colored parrots and tropical fish are examples of species evolving for millions of years in unchanging environments.

I speculate that our intelligence evolved using a sub category of what Darwin called "sexual selection", which we could call "selection by war". This concept can be explained using the intricate pattern on the peacocks' tail and comparing it to the human mind. The peacocks' tail evolved over millions of years as peahens selected their mates' based on the beauty of their potential mate's plumage. If a peacock didn't have a pretty tail it didn't survive to reproduce. Just as the plumage of the peacock is a major survival strategy, the mental capacity of primates is the predominant survival strategy. Modern recorded history is a chronicle of endless war. There is no reason to believe our ancestors in prerecorded history were any different. If the brains of one tribe can't outsmart the neighboring tribe the smaller brained males will lose the war and they will die before they get a chance to reproduce.

Some speculate that sapiens unlike other hominine species have the ability to combine their imagined realities into a superior social construct of language. Sapiens, over thousands of generations communicated their accumulated wisdom forming imagined realities and social constructs to organize and communicate with their soldiers. This tiny difference gave Sapiens an advantage over our close species cousins.

The outcomes of wars between tribal groups were decided on the intelligence and ingenuity of the winning tribes. We also know that man has a propensity to kill the males and take the women and children as slaves. This is also a survival strategy providing breeding females for the predominantly male conquering force. Intelligence would play a large role in who survives and what they look like. Beautiful women who put a lot of effort into their appearance would be the least likely to die in a battle between men. Men who were strong and cunning would be more likely to survive. The more intelligent victors would select the most beautiful remaining women thus the offspring would be more intelligent and more beautiful than the last generation. Over the last sixty thousand generations our brains have doubled in size and the beauty of our species has increased.

The question of why sapiens have no close cousins and what happened to Neanderthal and maybe a dozen other close species is easy to explain if one believes our intelligence came from the violent natural selection of conflict. We ethnically cleansed them out of existence just like we try to ethnically cleanse human beings, who are different in modern times, i.e.

(the murder of nine million people in the holocaust and twelve million in the Gulags of Siberia).

The value of a strong ruler who knows how to use social constructs to impose strict discipline on his warriors would obviously be an advantage. The ruler would also be the father of many off-spring from the women of the defeated tribes, thus most people today have ancestors who were rulers. According to a BBC documentary one out of every 200 people living on the planet today are directly related to Genghis Khan who apparently had sex (consensual?) with the most beautiful women of each conquered village.

If there is some truth in this theory it also answers the question of why some people, when given large amounts of political authority, become more amorous, malevolent and cruel. This cruel and diabolical intelligence is a survival strategy allowing the recipients of power to reproduce in great numbers. In a society that encourages rulers or gives individuals large amounts of authority there will be; more war, civil disturbance, draconian bureaucracy, taxes, formation of lawless ethnos and a lack of progress to improve people's quality of life. It will also be more difficult for the majority to pursue happiness.

On the other side of the coin there is a beautiful consequence to our intelligence. We have become great artists, innovators, builders, lovers and philosophers. In a democracy we understand each citizen is politically equal and we are motivated by status rather than power. We have learned how to consciously love. Our ancestors learned to survive by forming friendships and sharing resources. We developed systems to make laws giving us the freedom to live and love in prosperity. Our Athenian ancestors understood the nature of man well enough to encourage leadership and discourage the concept of (tyrant) ruler. Based on the concept of political equality, the Athenian's ever-changing citizens assembly managed for more than three hundred years to keep tyrants from forming factions in their law making assembly.

Democratic societies tend to dilute the amount of authority an individual can control. It is easy to find evidence in modern history to support this assumption by comparing democratic jurisdictions to societies that are burdened with dictators. Autocrats make decisions with questionable authority. Their decisions are often based on self-interest and giving privilege to friends and peers. Most times the laws made do not reflect the betterment of the overall population. Even if the laws improved the quality of life of the majority, there will remain a question in some people's minds about their legitimacy which will fuel an Ethnos. You might think dictators, because of their position, are free of oppression. The opposite is true. A dictator is oppressed by a need to continually put effort into oppressing the masses to a degree where they cannot organize opposition.

Athenian society discouraged the ruler and encouraged the concept of leader. The ancient Greeks built their government around the idea of preventing tyrants from taking over the assembly. The bi-nature is one of ruler or leader. A ruler uses authority to take taxes, resources and liberties by writing self-serving laws with questionable authority.

A leader is one who gives; gives of their love, their wisdom, their time, their organizational skills, and makes changes in society by leading people to consensus with legitimate authority. The citizen's assembly had the power to banish, for 10 years (ostracize, lose status in society) any member who could not stop themselves from demonstrating the characteristics of a ruler.

Because human nature has been crafted for a million years using a survival strategy of war we have been indoctrinated with the idea of following a ruler. Modern western societies from the organizational unit of the family to the highest government positions have this idea in their blood. We have been indoctrinated with the false assumption that the only way to make law is to give the ruling side of mankind authority over their more humble counterparts. In a representative democracy the only arresting feature from a full dictatorship is the thin benevolence of the elected officials and this can fail under stress as seen when democracies become dictatorships as demonstrated in Spain, Germany and Italy before the second Great War.

The world has never been the same since the people of Attica (ancient Greece) broke away from the tradition of using a ruler to make law. On the historical road from Attica to modern times our DNA has demanded we follow the ways of our violent ancestors. However numerous leaders in our recent past have been able to shed their genetic constraints and lead us into our modern democratic world.

The Concept of Citizen

Every human-being on the planet has inherited planetary citizenship from their ancestors. Almost all planetary citizens are represented by a UN delegate. There are few people who aren't citizens of a country and some have dual or multiple citizenship.

Citizenship usually implies privilege to a group of people who live in a part of the world (a country or jurisdiction). After the second Great War the UN was formed to maintain the established borders forming countries or jurisdictions.

Each country has its own unique set of rules. The citizen must obey the laws of their country and in return will have a set of rights and freedoms. Inside the jurisdiction of countries the idea that one citizen is better than another is extinguished with a set of rights and freedoms. All citizens are equal under the law. Apartheid in South Africa and laws against Jews in Nazi Germany were exceptions to this rule.

The negative side of citizenship is the concept of being a pawn, a worker, a taxpayer who belongs to a jurisdiction. It is possible to be oppressed by your nationality. An example is the Soviet Union imprisoning their citizens in the communist bloc countries. When you cross a border you are an alien. Countries restrict your activity; corporations exploit your nationality through currency exchange and providing services at inflated prices. The time away from your country is restricted. I personally know many Mexican citizens who feel like prisoners in their own country and I have read about millions who illegally seek the liberty of Western Society. Global participative democracy will remove the pressure to migrate by eliminating oppression. World citizens will find a place on the planet where they will be able to establish a solid foundation for future generations. Without oppression citizens will build unique traditions of art and science which will benefit the entire world.

It used to be a nightmare to travel in Europe because of the numerous border crossings and currency exchanges. European countries formed the EU taking away borders, checkpoints and having a common currency. Life is better and easier for citizens of Europe. With participative democracy citizens of the world will follow the example of the EU, eliminating borders but maintaining traditions.

When it comes to political authority all citizens have equal political authority when an election is in progress. After an election the citizen's political authority is given to an elected individual (President, Representative, Governor, Premier, or Prime Minister). Citizens have no control over their political authority after the winner of the political contest is decided. The citizens in a representative democracy rely solely on the benevolence of the elected oligarchy. Individuals and groups can only **influence** law makers. Between elections citizens control no political authority and must resort to whining, complaining and finger pointing while protesting in the rain in front of government offices.

Is there an argument to give the individual citizen equal political authority more than once every four years? It's obvious some people are more suited in today's world to lead. They have no fear of speaking in public, have a distinctive appearance, a mind that remembers clichés and bits of history and they give identity to a group. Before an election we give these individuals hero status and, unfortunately after their election, our authority.

Many of our non-elected citizens know far more than our elected officials about public issues and are more capable of thinking rationally. These quiet citizens are seldom heard. Their fear of speaking in public above the loud talking-heads in suits prevents their sensible solutions to problems from being heard. Our societies stumble along making tiny steps forward by trial and error, always treading on the edge with the possibility of collapse at any moment. There is no problem with a leader who has good council, and what better council is there than the total population?

Why should every citizen control the same amount of political authority from the age of consent until the end of life? If you exist on the planet today, you are special. Your ancestors had the correct traits to survive and reproduce with a fragile connection between each generation. Billions of individuals didn't survive. Each person who has a heart beating in their chest today is a winner in the amazing game of survival. You have the key to success locked away in your DNA. Because we exist in the biosphere of this planet, we are **equal,** and therefore the political authority to make laws for our future will be shared equally. The beautiful thing about each of us is a unique perspective for survival. Each person has a unique gift to share with citizens through our political system. If every individual controls exactly the same amount of political authority from the age of consent until death we will share these gifts that are necessary to create the best laws. The laws made by our future participative democracy will be spectacular. We are seven billion unique souls with unique solutions to problems. Participative democracy is the catalyst to render these billions of solutions into the very best most effective and efficient laws.

For the most part, the meaning of citizen has been stripped away in our western democracies. When the people of the world become true citizens, having ownership and responsibility in the laws made by our governments, we will not need bulky bureaucracies, huge judiciaries, massive police forces and expensive incarceration facilities. We will have good reason to trust our fellow citizens as we trust ourselves. No longer will we be able to blunt socially unacceptable behavior with excesses of money. Instead of money, happiness will be measured with status, good friends and respectful acceptance in the groups we choose to live within. Status, tolerance and respect will be king over money and greed.

Chapter 13   # Human traits

The human species by definition has sufficient diversity to survive environmental and social change. Within a large jurisdiction there is a full spectrum of all the traits of humanity, the most intelligent to the feeblest minded, some of us are musical, some not so much, funniest to humorless, most evil despot to kindest benevolent. It is wonderful to travel to experience the tastes and flavors of other cultures. It is also fun to note the similarities. It doesn't matter where you are you can find a group of street entertainers in the center of most major cities. The parents of jesters and mimes may disapprove of their children's occupations but somehow the traits their children acquired from their ancestors draw them to perform among masses of people. These individuals come from all aspects of society and are only the beginning of the similarities found in all civilizations. You will find the shopkeepers, the wholesalers, the doctors, nurses and other medical personnel, the builders and trades people, the educators, lawyers and politicians. Each one of these individuals has a combination of traits attracting them to the jobs they do well.

People find their specialty, just like the cells in the human body find their specialty as skin cells, liver cells or perhaps some very special cells in the retina of the eye. The Khmer Rouge of Cambodia murdering their professional people can be compared to the human body killing the specialist cells in the retina of the eye. The result is blindness causing the quality of our lives to diminish.

Only those who have not experienced other cultures, first hand, have the luxury of stereotyping people from other jurisdictions. This becomes apparent to those people who travel encountering a large variety of people, making the argument for stereotyping ridiculous. The traits we find in all cultures will form groups around their vested interests, regardless of the source of authority. There will be democrats, republicans, liberals, socialists and conservatives. In democratic western societies we have legalized this natural activity making it a right (The right to freedom of assembly). We are a whole people, we need every one of these traits found in our citizens and with this knowledge we can better ourselves, and the world we live in.

In order to understand how our democracies work we must understand the decision-making mechanisms within our jurisdiction. Again for simplicity a jurisdiction can be thought of as a group of people. This group can be defined as the people living inside a demographic area of land, i.e. a country, territory, state, province, county, town etc., or it could be a group based on a common interest, a belief system or a life style needing no defined demographic area. Jurisdictions are usually layered, each having authority over established components of society. For example federal governments may have authority over criminal law and fisheries, states or provinces may have authority over forestry and health and municipal governments may have authority over water and sewage. Within each jurisdiction there is a full spectrum of people.

Our diversity of moral values, our understanding of fair play and honesty shapes who we are. I once asked a lawyer friend what he did all day. How could he keep busy when people like me only see a lawyer for a few minutes a dozen times in their lives? He said, "Ninety five percent of the laws are made for five percent of the people. You are not part of that five percent. The five percent that keep me busy are the movers and shakers in society, the entrepreneurs, the politicians, and the people that run this country. These are my clients and they keep me busy from dawn till dusk."

Based on the increasingly stratified society we see around us there is truth in what he said. Some people are natural magnates who attract money. If you have money, you have power and privilege with the trickle down spin-off effect of improving the quality of life of the lower classes. For the last three decades England has attracted magnates by giving tax breaks to the wealthy with the expectation that this wealth will improve the quality of life of the British Citizen. The results of this experiment are unbelievably high real estate prices eliminating the possibility that the average British Citizen will ever own their own home. The British representative government seems powerless to do anything about it.

Stratification gives privilege to the five percent who are the ones running our political institutions and heavily influencing our law and policy making. In a representative democracy there is an unfair burden on taxpayers who must pay for the bureaucracies that make and manage complicated laws, rules and regulations. Magnates are essential just like all the other groups. However, in a participative democracy, the natural ratio of five percent is based on meritocracy and the benefits outweigh the negatives of a stratified society. In a participative democracy these magnates will need to not only terrify our politicians, by threatening to take their money to more friendly jurisdictions, but they will also need to convince citizens of their benevolence. In ancient Attica magnates took on huge responsibilities in exchange for privilege. Citizens demanded money for public projects, the arts, to pay for public education, social programs and in some cases entertainers, wine and food at festivals.

Without any outside encouragement people will form groups around their vested interests. Imagine the population in a participatory (representative) democracy as a teardrop on its side. Inside this teardrop is a smaller teardrop; the space between these teardrops represents all the people who don't want to participate. This group has been increasing as evidenced by poor turnouts for elections often more than 50%. The left side, or bulging part of the teardrop, represents what some people consider poor left wing bleeding heart socialists layabouts. Some valuable traits found in poor people often push them away from mainstream society and they find themselves in the left bulge. Frequently, brilliant artists, philosophers and novelists begin in the left bulge but more often it is the people who, for whatever reason, are marginalized by our meritocracy. Just as great wealth gives power and authority, poverty and lack of wealth gives great vulnerability. You see these people on the streets. Their hopes and dreams long ago dashed by failure. With psychologically thick skins they pick through the detritus of our society, competing with scavenging birds; food and comfort their only incentive.

One layer up, the young; exploited by pimps and drug lords in a lawless land, burn out their bodies, dreaming of a life that doesn't lead to homelessness. These people rarely participate in elections.

Above them, in the millions are the minimum wage workers who are perpetually poised on the edge of poverty. A slight sneeze in the economy will find them on the street with no work and no means of support. In good times you can find the marginally poor working three jobs in a desperate act to put their children through school.

Parents dream the dream of poverty-riddled children using their natural abilities to become wealthy. It is rare, but not unheard of for a child born in poverty to become extremely wealthy. In our fickle free market economy these stories of rags to riches are wonderful examples, used by the privileged, to justify how fair their system is. In a perfect world this statement could be true, if our free market economies were uncluttered with monopolies and privilege skewed towards the establishment.

The wealthy exploit these groups giving them work in their retail outlets, their factories and their farms. Often the profits from these enterprises find their way, into offshore bank accounts held by greedy plutocrats. The marginally poor are the backbone of our nations. Without this group western society would crumble.

The pointy part of the teardrop represents the wealthy, right wing autocrats. It is hard to know if this group is happy. The statistics are not good. Living secret lives in controlled estates, rarely venturing out in public, one can only speculate. People who meet them often report their surprise at finding them to be normal, friendly people. If you want to know their troubles, the paparazzi and society magazines can fill your head with stories and pictures of incredible oppression and unhappiness.

Many wealthy people try to improve their images, through philanthropy, by becoming great heroes of some cause or other. It can't be easy, cloistered in a world where you feel jailed by notoriety. It is said that great wealth and power come with great responsibility. Without this group our civilization would crumble.

Both the very poor and the very wealthy have strong influence over our elected oligarchies through advocacy groups. The political lefts have their unions and advocates while the political right has their lobbyists.

The middle of the teardrop represents the hard working, taxpaying citizens who don't have the money or time to lobby government. Most of these people are alive with brilliant ideas but under the oppressive corporate leash they struggle for a sense of self-worth by hurriedly discussing issues of government, industry, sometimes sex, cars and bad bosses in their trips to and from work with strangers or on their ten-minute coffee breaks. Their days are filled with unending repetition. A career that starts out as fun and fulfilling over decades becomes a burden, burning away their creative energies. Most live in a rut or what is known as their comfort zone. They must work to pay their bills and feed their children. Most feel they have no ownership or responsibility in the decisions made by government and have given up caring.

The middle class watch their family values erode as runaway corporate social engineering (advertising) influence fills their children with sentiment. You can see them walking the busy streets, lonely empty shells, seeking anonymity and finding solace in over-consumption. They find it hard to associate with other people without the help of alcohol or prescribed mind-altering drugs. Living in a chemical haze of caffeine and alcohol and finding little joy in reality, they seek the fantasy found on the internet or in movies.

It is increasingly difficult to stimulate this group into participating when they know they have no influence or effect on the decisions made by government. Electronic devices and schedules dominate their lives, separating them from the joys of family and friends. The middle class is the meat in the sandwich between the wealthy and the poor. If you are wealthy you don't need to be a lawyer, engineer or accountant. You hire them and use them to control the masses. Without the middle class our civilization would crumble.

In our western society we have all the ingredients for happiness with one exception. We've little or no sense of ownership or responsibility, no sense of control or security. Many of us live in fear and ignorance generated by our unrealistic media, who successfully spin small tragedies into earthshaking scenarios of doom, all for the almighty buck. The pursuit of happiness is so exploited by our corporations in their business of extracting wealth from the garden of unhappy citizens that they become blind to their greed and believe the advertising lies they spin.

Democracy and the Party System

In the inner teardrop a relatively small number of people form groups around their vested interests, creating political parties. In smaller jurisdictions where people have more of a sense of ownership and responsibilities, political parties are not formalized. Groups form around candidates that represent their vested interests.

Within the political party a leader is elected. The leader has great influence, but no more authority than any other card carrying member. Decisions regarding policy or resolutions to issues are done at the party convention level through a democratic vote. In theory each card-carrying member controls exactly the same amount of political authority within the party. The decisions are made using a form of participative democracy where it is know exactly what the level of consensus is. Policy and resolutions made in this way at convention are legitimate, because they have a consensus of the party members behind them.

Most people in our western civilization have been indoctrinated with one form of democracy; representative democracy (participatory). This is a system where we impose a ruling group of people (oligarchy) upon ourselves for a limited period of time. This oligarchy comes from the political party system. After election, the leader of the winning political party becomes a ruler and is little different from a king or queen having the ultimate authority to make law for the jurisdiction.

The way this oligarchy obtains and maintains this political authority is through a competitive struggle for political support within an electoral process. This electoral process was established hundreds of years ago. We have no political engineers to build a better system so we must struggle on with this old, tired and very inefficient system. It's too bad we don't have a better system because our political authority is very quickly being replaced with the authority of well-engineered corporations.

Participative democracy changes the shape of society from a tear drop on its side to a round ball filled with political equality and fairness. There is no recognition of race, color, gender, religion or politics. Political equality is guaranteed to all human beings that have a heart beating in their chest and are of the age of consent. Participative democracy insures laws are made with legitimacy. Legitimate laws do not carry the burden of oppression. This lifting of oppression from our political systems will change the mind-set of our citizens giving us a better perspective on life which in turn will lift all citizens into a fulfilling positive world.

Chapter 15

The Electoral Process

Today, in a representative democracy elections are a game of winners and losers. The poor citizen is expected to make a decision about who will be the best representative. This of course is an impossible task because no one can predict what a government will do in the period of their mandate. Many citizens vote to get rid of the last government at all costs by choosing the least objectionable group.

The laws or legislations produced by government become less important than the personalities of the contestants. If you want to win, the number of votes cast in your favor must be greater than the opponents'.

The first step within the political party is the election of a leader, someone with the correct charisma, charm and voter appeal. They must have the ability to speak and argue the point for the vested interests of the party-members without offending non-committed citizens. Good hair and youth are important. Remember half the voters are the opposite sex of the leader so make sure the leader is good looking and has enough sex appeal and voter recognition. Good-looking people are more likely to be elected.

The party must provide a platform promising logical reasons to elect the candidate. Problems, needs, and issues, common within the electorate must be identified. This platform may need to be changed mid-election to accommodate the party's impression of their chances of winning and so it should be kept vague and open to interpretation.

Researching the history and foibles of the opposing candidates is a necessary ingredient in winning an election. The information gathered is used to smear the opposition, twisting their words and making them appear to be morons by broadcasting propaganda through the media. The political candidates must know the art of not answering questions. When a question is asked they should respond with a question or defer the answer by talking about an entirely different subject. All politicians seeking elected office, if they have any intention of winning, are familiar and well-practiced in the art of double-speak or baffle-gab. Honesty and straight answers are often a ticket to disaster.

Early in the process an election advisory committee consisting of managers of research, publicity, contacts, etc. is formed. This is where the hard work begins. To identify support party members are handed voters lists and asked to go through the thousands of names identifying possible supporters. The candidate and other representatives of the party begin a systematic door-to-door campaign throughout the jurisdiction and attend all public political gatherings.

The contact committee works on the citizen lists, social media pages and computer generated data finding supporters and identifying level of support, usually by phone. Strong supporters are given an opportunity to give financially and to identify other supporters. Undecided and non-supporters are recorded. Wall charts with each voter's number need to be produced identifying known support.

On voting day scrutinizers working for each party at the polling station record the voters as they vote. The information is delivered to campaign headquarters where each voter is marked off on the chart. A few hours into the election, known supporters that haven't voted are phoned and reminded that it's voting day. To get voters to the polling place transportation is offered by the election committee. Getting your vote out is the most important part of running a successful campaign.

In Participatory democracy (representative democracy), the period of time between the date the election is declared, (the writ is dropped) and the day the winner is announced, usually a month or more, is a time when all citizens control exactly the same amount of political authority at that level of government. The billionaire and the guy who works in the Quickie Mart, both only have one vote. In ancient Greece citizens controlled exactly the same amount of political authority (participative democracy) from the age of consent until death. In a representative democracy citizens have no control of their POPA for the term of government, (two to five years). In Attica there was never a time when the citizen did not control political authority. This condition existed for more than 300 years (512BC to 198BC) and is the foundation for our modern society.

The election is a competitive struggle between the political parties to win the approval of the most number of participating citizens or first past the post, winner take all. After the election the leader of the winning political party controls the bulk of political authority in the elected oligarchy. This oligarchy is externalized from the people and it no longer requires any approval from the citizens to change laws or enact bills or legislation. In the British Parliamentary System the head of the oligarchy, (The Prime Minister or Premier) can only be overruled by the House of Lords, (Canadian Senate) or Sovereign or appointee of the Sovereign, the Lieutenant Governor. These positions are largely ceremonial giving an unlimited mandate to the winner of the political contest. The elected official-opposition and all other citizens only have influence. All political authority is taken by the winning political party and given to the leader of the political party who becomes the head of the jurisdiction.

Although in the US federal congress, (comprising the house of representatives and the senate), one can find many checks and balances there is still a large disconnect between the citizens and the laws generated by this institution. Although a president and cabinet can put a bill before congress their powers are limited to signing and vetoing legislation.

With very few exceptions more than fifty percent of the population is not represented in representative government. Because there is no official way of measuring the quantity of approval from the general citizenship, for any decisions made in the mandate of the elected government, the authority used to make law should be considered questionable, fueling ethnos, increasing bureaucracies, and government debt.

Most western democracies have some form of direct democracy. Incentives, propositions, referendums and recall processes. All are crude attempts to involve the general population in decision-making. In most cases they do work and they definitely get the population involved. However, small vested interest groups wanting to manipulate the law in their favor often exploit direct democracy to gain privilege. There is no engineering in the process, and the decisions from these processes are fraught with perils through their wording and timing. The outcomes are often opposite the original objective, but somehow are now written in stone because the people have spoken. A good example of the perils of these crude forms of direct democracy can be seen in "Brexit" the referendum in the UK to separate from the EU. Did the people of Great Britain, who have had no practice in participative democracy, achieve their goals with this referendum?

Participative democracy is a solution to the growing frustration in citizens living in Western Societies.

Chapter 16

Guns and Liberty

Participative democracy will end the need for guns. The biggest threat to civil society is inequality. When a group is given privilege, by definition there must be an underprivileged group. The American constitution's second amendment (the right of the people to keep and bear arms, shall not be infringed.) is a provision granting all citizens, whether they be police, military or common citizens' equality in the use of deadly force.

To minimize the number of guns we make laws restricting numbers and regulating use. The NRA recognizes danger comes when a part of society is given the privilege to own and control deadly weapons and another part of society is denied the same privilege.

With the advent of recording devices it becomes clear police and military personal controlling deadly force are no different than anyone else. In cases, when the person holding the weapon (citizen, police or military) judge they are being threatened they will shoot first and think later. Governments who have given military personnel and police the privilege of carrying and controlling instruments of deadly force, while restricting the same for their citizens are oppressive. The United States was built on the concept of liberty and therefor to avoid oppression; if police and military personal are given the privilege of carrying arms and using deadly force so must every citizen.

The best answer is equality. No one including, police or military should ever carry instruments of deadly force. We all know guns are unnecessary, solve nothing and in fact exacerbate violence. I know the majority of enforcement officers would gladly give up their guns if they knew there were no instruments of deadly force in their jurisdiction. In the past the British bobby carried something more powerful than a gun. They carried the authority of the Crown. When police officers carry the authority of a legitimate government, the most powerful authority we have ever known, there will be no need for guns.

The second option to controlling guns while not stomping on liberty is to find consensus in the mass of the people. Legitimate law made with consensus from the people is the most powerful element when it comes to controlling the production and use of guns. It is time to have an open and free debate between groups with different solutions to controlling these instruments of deadly force.

Today we need guns because we live in oppressive societies where governments use questionable authority to make law. If there is no oppression there is no need for guns. In the next few generations our offspring will form participative democracies creating an environment of liberty where open and free debate is possible and more than enough legitimate authority will be available to end oppression and the need for guns.

Participative democracy will end war. Historically it is hard to find an international conflict started by the common people. It is easy to find wars started by heads of state that control political authority. In good wars we have needed a powerful military to protect our sovereignty and our way of life. However, the justifications for training, putting a uniform on a person and sending them across a border where it is legal to kill, are many. Millions of precious lives have been lost to satisfy the ego of a megalomaniac tyrant who has the political authority and the ability to oppress masses of people with their psychopathic imagined reality of grandeur. The truth is wars are usually started by a few bloody-minded heads of state in a pissing contest with other heads of state. Wars don't make any sense to the common citizens who know their children could become cannon fodder, especially women. This means war will end when women control the making of law through their numbers.

War is a legal entity. Any nation can create an army and declare war on another nation. There is no law against it. And we know all is fair in war and that is when the veneer of civilization disappears.

In the environment of liberty in our western societies few young men take the lives of others. In order to make an effective fighting force it is necessary to change this attitude of peace. It is the same with any species. Your family dog, if treated poorly, could easily be changed into a vicious, biting attack dog. In boot camp our young people are put in an environment of extreme oppression. For a period of six weeks or more the subject is stripped of any ownership or responsibility. They are verbally and physically abused and in some cases are hazed by their fellows. The sad thing is, nations that don't strip their soldiers of self-determination lose battles.

In a state of war soldiers know that if they disobey an order or desert, they will be punished by incarceration or even death as per military law. They know that if they are given an order to kill the enemy of their oppressors and refuse they will die. The chance of glory and survival is greater if they kill the so called enemy even though in different circumstances the so called enemy could become a good friend.

The comment "a veteran with psychological problems" is often heard on news stories after the veteran has slaughtered innocent citizens. The moniker, shell shock in the first war, battle fatigue in the second and PTSD today describe a life-long torment for soldiers who have experienced battle. However the psychological injuries suffered by soldiers often don't occur when encountering the enemy but rather are the results of oppression inside the military.

The contrast between killing a person in your own jurisdiction to that of being a soldier killing a person in a foreign land is extreme. One is tried for murder and put away for life, the other is welcomed home as a hero. The veneer of civilization quickly dissolves in war exposing the black side of humanity. War is a type of insanity. There is no argument or justification for war!

Is it possible the solution to ending war is as simple as making an international law saying war is illegal? In a participative democracy I can see a group starting up on Facebook consisting of millions of mostly women, who want to stop war. They find some UN delegates of the same mind and then solicit a billion planetary citizens to move their POPA (piece of political authority) to the delegates who want to end war. The pressure on the UN would be tremendous with international media coverage. A news story announcing a law to end war will be celebrated by the entire world.

Countries are just like people. They want to go about their business without interference. Countries interfere with each other ultimately leading to war. Imagine an international law stating, "Without UN sanction the head of state of a nation who sends an intrusive force across their border into a foreign nation or uses their forces to kill their own people is responsible for any death as the result of their action." Perhaps UN forces would be responsible for hunting down and trying in an international court, perpetrators who break this law, just as Nazi war criminals were treated. Can you think of anything more satisfying than finding Vladimir Putin, George W. Bush and Benjamin Netanyahu being found guilty of breaking this international law? It would be hard to find a head of state from any country who would risk having their name put on a list of wanted criminals.

Legitimate law is a powerful thing. In Attica (ancient Greece) no nation, no individual, or group of individuals could overrule the laws made by the citizens' assembly. The legitimate authority of a modern participative democracy using the world population will be the most powerful authority imaginable. The institution of war will surely decline and ultimately end.

One of the greatest failures of our democracies and our free market economy is the uncontrolled extraction of our natural resources. Participative democracy will stop the unneeded extraction of natural resources and build a sustainable environment. Part of our survival strategy is competing for food and shelter. If we find something useful in nature we use it first before someone else does. Our normal response to seeing a fish is to catch it and eat it. If we know there is only one fish left we justify taking it because, if we don't, someone else will.

There is good evidence to suggest our tribal ancestors did not have the same attitude. In fact they had ceremonies to preserve natural resources. Over thousands of years and many generations, they developed a collective wisdom. Our ancestors worshiped the Bios as a currency just as we idolize money. They knew they had to protect the Bios by co-operating or their people would die.

In Western Culture the wisdom of our elders is diluted by technology and our new god; **money**. We don't have the wisdom of past generations and no sense of ownership or responsibility for the future of our natural environment. Our collective wisdom is strangled by top down forces telling us what to do and how to think. The last fish syndrome is very quickly using up the biosphere's natural resources as caring people like Dr. David Suzuki burn out trying to use our ancient political system to make necessary change.

As western societies close down our industries and export jobs to third world countries, where the source of authority is not the people, we survive by selling our non-renewable resources to dictatorships. This is an example of the last fish syndrome. We, the people of western society, know this is wrong and that it will cause great harm in the future, but we have no ownership or responsibility for this process. Therefore the harm will be done.

Because the political cycle is short, the incentive to make laws with long term solutions is diluted. Politicians worry about solving problems happening in their four to five-year term in office and leave future problems for the next batch of politicians. These shortsighted laws, made without wisdom, put the future of our biosphere in jeopardy.

Chapter 19

Isms, Ocracies and Evolution

Charles Darwin observed the changing diversity of species in the Bios and composed his theory of diversity and natural selection. It is possible to observe the Demos through history, recognizing political patterns of survival.

This work is not about isms it is about **ocracies**. Isms can be thought of as; the brand of car (Ford or Chevy), the names of political groups (Democrat or Republican), political philosophies which often come with a manifesto, code of ethics and sometimes a bible. This work is not about isms, it is about **ocracies** or the source of authority to make law. Inside an **ocracy** like democracy one can find elements of capital**ism**, social**ism**, Catholic**ism**, Buddh**ism**, Muhammad**ism** and even communal**ism**. **Ocracy** is the driving force. The question; is the mechanism to make law powered by horses (our two hundred year old representative democracy), an internal combustion engine or an electric motor? **Ism** is the diversity of thought, the style that makes up a robust and healthy society.

In the first millennium before Christ in Western Europe Rome, Greece and Marseilles experimented with forms of **democracy** starting as Greek city states. Athenian radical **democracy** was absorbed into the Roman republic in 198 BC. The authority of the Roman republic was eroded and replaced with **autocracy** in 44BC with the emperors of Rome. In a little less than 400 years the authority of **autocracy** was eroded by the **theocracy** of the Roman church. **Theocracy** was eroded and replaced with **Aristocracy** in the Renaissance. **Aristocracy** was eroded and replaced by **democracy** after the French Revolution. Representative **democracy** is being eroded and replaced with **plutocracy** at the beginning of the twenty-first century.

Rather than destroying old traditions of authority Western Europe has preserved democratic ideas from ancient Greece and the Republic of Rome, the Catholic Church and the Monarchies of Europe.

It is rare to see jurisdictions that preserve the traditions of ocracys from their past. Western European countries are the exception preserving the traditions from as far back as the medieval period. These traditions form a broad foundation under their democracies. In an intolerant, knee-jerk action jurisdictions like Russia and China have wiped out the foundations holding up their fragile source of authority. More important than the oppression this causes in their people, it is also a threat to world stability.

At this time in history if my contemporaries do nothing our descendants may never experience the plethora of benefits potentially available from a participative democracy. Already the wealthy are strangling our large cities with ownership. Our politicians sit back and watch plutocrats acquire property to rent. Our young people are losing hope of ever owning their own home. Greece is leading the parade of countries lined up to sell their assets to plutocrats eroding the authority of their elected governments into powerless puppet governments.

If done properly participative democracies will preserve and tolerate the traditions of our present representative (participatory) democracy along with traditions of the monarchies and theocracies like Roman Catholicism and Islamic belief systems. It will also preserve the valuable role of magnates in our society. The citizens of ancient Attica used the natural traits of magnates to pay for all manor or wonderful capital projects, art and public festivals.

In Plato's "Allegory of the Cave", he describes the watery vision we all have about the true nature of forms. Some interpret his allegory as describing the effects of education and the lack of it on our nature. Truth based on sentiment controls our world. In so many ways if enough people know something to be true then we *believe*, and in our minds it is true (social constructs). Behavior scientists (social engineers) recognize our cognitive abilities. Money, corporations, and religions are classified as imagined realities, social constructs and legal fictions. Logic dictates that money, corporations and religions are figments of our imagination and yet in our minds nothing could be further from the truth.

It is not hard to find people who do not believe we are part of the animal kingdom and it is not hard to find this type of sentiment in the works of our advertisers, spin-doctors, politicians and in the tall tales told by our friends and neighbors. Keep in mind how bland our lives would be if we only told the truth. Life would be like spaghetti sauce with no oregano, so boring without the spice of embellishment and little white lies.

Among other things, Athenian citizens judged the truth of speakers of the citizen's assembly. Even if the speaker was honest and correct, if two hundred and fifty citizens judged the speaker's words as false, they would write the name of the speaker on a pot shard and place the "ostracon" in the box at the entrance to the assembly. If more than two hundred and fifty ostracons with the same name were deposited a council of elders (Council of 500) was charged with the task of arranging a court case to try the accused speaker. Lying, obstruction and cheating at the assembly was taken seriously. Depending on the importance of the case the jury could consist of up to five hundred and one citizens. The accused would get three chances to prove their innocence. The court consisted of advocates on both sides of the question having an open and free debate trying to convince the jury of guilt or innocence. The process was designed to find truth. If the court found the speaker guilty of misleading citizens or obstructing the business of the citizens' assembly (ecclesia) their citizenship would be removed and they would be banished or ostracized from the citizen's assembly for a period of ten years. Modern courts and ancient Athenian tribunals function differently but the motivation in both is to find truth.

It is difficult, if not impossible, to find real truth; however, by using the concepts of **discovery** and **creation** it is possible to sort out what is in fact truth from man-made imagined realities and social constructs. If we assume everything has already been created then the only thing left is to discover it. Scientists discover truth, by using scientific method; they propose theories, set up experiments to prove their claims and then send their methods and results to other scientists. If enough other scientists get the same results, the theory becomes truth. The hazard in our modern world is that corporations own their scientists and all the results they produce and are thus able to hide truth on items that are not profitable or undermine the credibility of the corporation.

Our Bios is filled with living things that are not our imagined realities. Today we are scratching the surface of understanding of our Bios by observing and uncovering fundamental truths about our natural world. Often the harder we look the more we realize our depth of ignorance. However discoveries are made and with equivocation we can say they are true. The atom bomb is true, the internal combustion engine is true and yet man did not create them, we discovered them. If we assume a supreme being created everything then we can say scientists are closer to God than priests because scientists discover truth whereas spiritual leaders create truth through imagined realities and social constructs.

Truth, in art, can be defined as discovering things that are already there. Michelangelo saw his David in the block of marble when it was laying half carved by a different sculptor. He apparently said he discovered his David by removing the stone around it. When we read a story or a history we can assume the story was not discovered, man created it. What you're reading now was created by me, therefore it is, at best, questionable truth.

Western society was built on a concept from Athenian society we call a system of reference. In one of Pericles's speeches he says, "When you speak to the Assembly, you do so at your peril." By this he meant it was necessary to prove what you said was true, or the citizens would ostracize you and take away your citizenship. Aristotle was one of many who wrote reference books used by the leaders of Athens to prove they were speaking the truth. In scientific literature you will find a bibliography referencing the work to previous known truths.

Science, law, medicine and politics all rely on this system of reference to determine truth. Written truth is often a threat to autocrats. China, until recently, oppressed truth just as the Romans burned the books of Alexandria. It is important to allow freedom of expression to expose truth and allow our world to move toward sustainability. In Western society we have legalized freedom of expression (the right to Freedom of Speech). One way to find clarity in an issue is open and free debate among leaders of our society. To be effective open and free debate must include a broad spectrum of interested citizens.

What happened in the past cannot be changed. The problem is, there are as many truths to a story as there are people to tell it. There is only one history; however our scholars have created a written history from the perspective of the victors in great historical conquests. As students we learn the names of hundreds of great warlords: Alexander the Great, Augustus Cesar, Mark Anthony, and Adolph Hitler. These histories come from the pens of men employed by the winners, so one would expect them to write favorably about their masters and negatively about their enemies. We call this propaganda. Written histories are difficult to preserve for long periods because paper turns to powder after a few hundred years. Histories must be written on media that can be preserved or if on paper they must be copied. Copies are subject to editing, so it is difficult to tell how accurate the copies are. Much of the history of ancient Greece has been learned from writings on pieces of original ceramic pots.

To find the best solutions to problems in our societies we need the truth and the best way to find it is through open and free debate. As citizens we will learn from our mistakes and move towards consensus on the best solutions to problems. Because representative politics is filled with secrecy and unearned political authority the results are often flawed, causing increased complexity and bureaucracy.

In business we don't mind spending large sums of money on lawyers and accountants to ensure honesty and we have been indoctrinated to trust politicians rather our neighbors to have anything to do with making law. If our ancestors living inside a tribal groups perceived strangers as a threat then we can assume in modern times we struggle against a built in distrust of strangers. In a global participative democracy we will be teem members in a single tribe where each citizen controls equal political authority eliminating our distrust in strangers and naturally encouraging social interaction.

The British used this distrust to divide and conquer great nations, just as our establishment encourages this distrust to preserve their privileged position. Our world is filled with security systems to protect us from ourselves. The sad thing is that this distrust is the critical element hampering us from saving the world. In our economic system we have accountants to foster trust and likewise in our political system we need political engineers to account and make fair our political system.

According to Sir Moses Finley the people of ancient Attica trusted each other. In one of Pericles's funeral speeches you can find the words "We can cast open our doors and have no fear because we can trust the stout hearts of our fellow citizens".

Imagine sometime in the early part of the twenty-first century some super rich CEOs of internet companies decide there is some merit to expanding their software to fulfill the fundamental principle of democracy by giving each citizen the ability to control their POPA from the age of consent until the end of life. The incentive for the software companies is to increase the number of users, making their software even more valuable.

Like so many bits of social media the platform will be a surprise, not realized until we find it entrenched all around us. The developers believe even if there is no reason to predict a cataclysmic end, our world will be a better place if we enjoy legitimate laws. The developers decides to build simple interface- able platforms giving each citizen of the world the ability to see who is using their POPA based on the demographic location of the citizen's home address.

This simple platform is entirely citizen controlled. The individual, if they choose can join giving sufficient information to establish their identity as a planetary citizen. Politicians have the option of joining and using the provided platform to broadcast their beliefs and policies.

After joining the citizen sees their political account. They see which politicians are using their POPA to make law. The citizen can also see lists of politicians who are competing with their politician at the same level of government. The citizen can find the politician's record and policies by reviewing what each politician has posted.

If the citizen doesn't like what their politician is doing

they can hover their finger over the green dot representing their POPA. When the green dot starts to blink the citizen moves their finger dragging their POPA to a politician who represents their vested interests. The change is recorded on a secure server similar to the ones used by our banks.

By accounting the number of citizens each politician represents, an absolute number representing percentage of consensus can be generated for each law passed.

The citizen will see which politicians are using their political authority to make law on a municipal level, a state, territorial or provincial level, a federal level and who their UN delegate is. The citizen is in control. They decide when they go into their secure isolated virtual political account. Citizen's see what politicians have posted and move their political authority if they choose without prejudice just as we do today with our bank accounts.

Yikes? Will the establishment run around shouting "the sky is falling!" like they did after Adam Smith published his book "The Wealth of Nation" in 1764? Will modern aristocracy insist on making laws to hunt down supporters of this seditious instrument?

Probably not; my guess is politicians will welcome a new stage. Just as they have embraced social media, politicians will go into high gear trying to attract as many followers as possible.

It will be interesting to watch elected governments scrap over the percentage of consensus results from the internet service. If there is a question of legitimacy, when say a law is passed with only ten percent consensus, the opposition will use the information to discredit the government, the winners will denounce the information and the media will use the information as part of a story. It won't be long before governments start tailoring their legislations in a competitive struggle to get a percentage of consensus over fifty percent. Political groups led by common citizens who have a specialty and understand better than any politician the unforeseen consequences of present or proposed laws will form. Unlikely people who love to analyze documents will become leaders. Our governments will be under a microscope.

I can't wait to hear the debate about rightful and legitimate government. I can't wait to listen to clear and open debates for and against new laws and reforms. However, it will be hard to get away from the incessant crowing of angry roosters with comb over hairdos. The good news is, these roosters, with all their finery, will be harmless because, as citizens, we know we can rely on the stout hearts of our fellow citizens.

Yes citizens will realize they are the center, they are in control. Global citizens will realize they form a round political world with politicians revolving around them. This is in contrast to the present idea of a flat political earth extending to the boundaries of our own country with citizens orbiting around politicians. Over a decade or two people will realize this universal political power is a beautiful thing capable of making the best law for all. The world will slowly change as people compete for status by being the absolute best citizens.

We will be able to live without keys. War will be a thing of the past. World population will fall leaving enough resource to allow nature to re-balance. We will change our border crossings into welcome centers. We will have meaningful lives with twenty hour flex schedule work weeks and we will meter our resources making only the best most resilient products.

Our world will be free of Machiavellian political thought where potential rulers have morphed into honest caring leaders who get things done using the powerful authority of our citizens.

Oh yes, our world will be a wonderful environment of **liberty** filled with competition to live the best, think the best, build the best and give the most. Our international laws will be simple and crystal clear crafted with the power of a billion minds with ownership and responsibility in each and every law.

Can you imagine living in the year 2100 and looking back at the year 2018? If we do the correct things now, our descendants might be in a position to consider us politically primitive. You might hear a schoolteacher of the future talking about the injustices of the past just as we talk of the slavery one hundred and fifty years ago or the lack of democracy for women and landless people. The history books of the future might tell of a time when citizens of our time didn't control their POPA, had no right to food, shelter and no right to health and welfare. Our descendants might criticize our society because people in the prime of their lives worked far too many hours, not because they wanted to but because they needed to, to survive. Our descendants will study the histories of governments producing laws which unknowingly served the criminal ethnos who supplied prostitutes and unregulated drugs at inflated prices to a desperate uneducated public. They will read about fabulously wealthy drug lords who went to war with governments while established governments went to war with other countries because of their lust for oil.

Future teachers might have difficulty convincing their students of how lucky they are because they can walk freely to their unlocked homes and talk to strangers without fear. The children of the future, knowing no other world, will have trouble imagining how their ancestors, from the beginning of the twenty-first century could have possibly lived in a world of paranoia, over work, crime and hate?

To change our political systems we need political engineers to update and improve efficiency. Our universities must immediately begin the process of recruiting people to teach political engineering. These people will have the knowledge of political systems and the will to begin the process of safely moving to a citizen-driven political system. Fundamental principles and a code of ethics will be established using the knowledge of political scientists. Perhaps we will find the principles from ancient Attica useful. Clistenese's proclamation of 508 BC used fundamental democratic principles.

1. No new laws can be made unless all citizens have access to the system and control exactly the same amount of political authority.

2. No individual or group of people can contest the decisions of the citizens' political system.

One of the most important subjects in Athenian schools was politics. The day after a young man became a citizen at the age of eighteen he was expected to be able to run the citizens' assembly.

We need to enlighten our children by teaching political principles in public schools. We must impart every child with the certainty that they are politically equal. Every child must be indoctrinated with the idea that they have inherited from their ancestors a piece of political authority POPA. When students reach the age of consent they will understand the principles of authority, the various forms of government and they will know they have ownership and responsibility in making law with their inherited POPA. Many will know how to establish a legitimate decision in a group by being able to run a dispute resolving mechanism.

Students must understand the principles of spin, the artful manipulation of our reality, the psychology of propaganda, the cognitive ideas of social constructs, imagined realities and legal fictions. We must be able to practice manipulation so that we can all be on a level playing field when it comes to understanding how groups work the system to give themselves privilege.

Students must know what their charter of rights and freedoms mean and what their responsibilities are if they want to maintain these rights and freedoms. Our schools should foster trust and tolerance between students and the adults they associate with.

The biggest day of a young person's life will be the day they become citizens, the day they give up their sponsored citizenship and take on the responsibilities of participating in the making of law. This is the day they can honestly say they have ownership in their community, their state, territory or province, their federal government and the biosphere of the planet earth through the UN. This is the special day when the responsibility for the future of mankind and the biosphere of our planet falls directly into their hands.

It is a good thing to know the names of past presidents or prime ministers but it is not as important as knowing the sequential struggle for rights and freedoms and what these rights and freedoms mean to our quality of life. What is suffrage and how did the people of the past obtain the right to vote for a representative? Who were the suffragettes and what did they go through to win the right to vote? Believe me, the great heroes of the past were not only the prime ministers or presidents but also the common people who had the courage to stand up to the elite who ran our governments.

In ancient Greece, Solon's reform in 594 BC and Cleisthenes' reform in 508 BC were intended to create industry and reduce the problems of tyrants forming factions in Attica. Participative Democracy gave each male over the age of 18 who was not a slave something in common. They had political equality at the citizens' assembly.

The leaders of factions and would be autocrats were not left out. Like every other citizen, if they could gain enough support, they could further their cause at the assembly. In this way the interests of minority groups moved toward the majority group and the majority group moved toward the minority group in a process of moving towards consensus. In order to control people wanting to cheat and manipulate the citizen's assembly the laws governing the workings of the assembly were constantly being modified. The use of the ostracon and a lottery system to randomly select which citizen would serve as director of the assembly, were changes put in place to stop corruption and obstruction in the citizen's assembly. Our modern system of government has remained static resulting in corporate tyrannies and obstruction.

In theory, each citizen in the present time controls exactly the same amount of political currency giving us something in common, but only over the term of an election. In a participative democracy citizens control their piece of political authority twenty-four seven, three hundred and sixty five days a year. To influence law in a participative democracy lobbyists and special interest groups will need to appeal to the population of interested citizens not to government ministers in secret closed rooms.

There is a need to improve our present government. We now have Democracy 1.0. The new version will be 1.1. Think of using a 200-year-old system of transportation in our modern world; we would be up to our eyes in horse manure, or using DOS 1.0 today. It works, but man is it is awkward and slow. Representative democracy in our modern world can be compared to a horse and buggy going down a freeway filled with vehicles going seventy miles an hour. Not only is our antiquated political system dangerous but it is also inefficient, ineffective and extremely expensive.

There is a need to utilize the untapped resource, our people, in decision making; (just as we do in our free market economy) thus coming up with the best decisions that need little bureaucracy or policing.

There is a need to stop minority groups, like unions and corporations, from steering our government into making laws that favor their minorities.

There is a need to give non-political experts in our society the chance to make positive change by letting them supply political parties with the best solutions.

There is a need for our elected officials to compete with each other for citizen's support just as the producers of goods and services in our free market economy compete for customers. No longer will politicians sit back after winning an election knowing they wield political power for their remaining term in office. An elected official who promotes laws benefiting the overall good will get instant feedback and authority from citizens. In a true participative democracy where citizens choose who to give their POPA to, twenty-four seven, three hundred and sixty-five days a year, the good politician will control real political authority rather than just influence in lawmaking.

There is a need to make the job of being the people's representative more pleasant and rewarding. Politicians will have a real job of listening, producing solutions, and selling concepts to their constituents. They will earn the authority (by proxy) of citizens who have confidence in them. Because politicians will no longer be seen as dictators arbitrarily making ridiculous laws to satisfy minority groups, citizens will develop a deep respect and love for their politicians, similar to the great heroes of ancient Greece.

There is a need for honesty, integrity and openness from politicians. If we want the most effective and efficient laws, citizens need access to everything that goes on in government. We must end the secrecy behind closed doors in in-camera meetings. This will increase integrity in our political leaders. The more integrity and public trust, the more political power a representative will have in the form of proxy. In this system a politician who has no support from the electorate will have the equivalent authority of one citizen when voting for or against legislations. If he or she has the trust of tens of thousands he or she will control tens of thousands of pieces of political authority.

There is a need to change the attitudes of citizens and politicians by giving both citizens and politicians equal ownership and responsibility in the formation of law. No longer will people be able to point fingers and complain about the stupidity of politicians. The responsibility for any and all unforeseen consequences or problems resulting from bad laws will be shared equally between each citizen, not just a few politicians.

There is a need to utilize the recommendations of the advocates of representative democracy, by retaining a strong, expert minority to lead us. At the same time we must use the recommendations of the advocates of participative democracy to truly give each individual citizen, equality in law-making.

There is a need for governments and citizens to move together. Today the citizen and the government are far apart and moving away from each other. Participative Democracy bonds the two together because of the direct input from citizens.

There is a need to remove any chance a decision will be made, not for the betterment of the citizens, but because the winner of a political contest arbitrarily want to destroy what the opposition had accomplished in the previous government.

There is a need to make laws where no individual, group, or powerful corporation can influence or question the laws made by a participative democracy. Governments of today are rapidly losing authority due to international and domestic pressure from corporations.

There is a need to move away from absolute faith in money. Participative democracy will form a new type of currency. Status and true respect will be more important than money.

There is a need to move away from the "Best in Show" type of elections. In a representative democracy the outcome of elections is the most import part of democracy. In a participative democracy the most important part is the product of politics, the actual laws produced by government.

People have been increasingly voting for the least evil. I've seen polls showing the most popular Republican, in this case Donald Trump, showing a rating of people who would never vote for him, of sixty-eight percent. The other candidates had a slightly less unwanted rating. In a participative democracy, as long as full spectrums of candidates are elected, it really doesn't matter who gets elected.

There is a pressing need to **solve the problem of overpopulation** without using oppressive methods. Since the third decade of the twentieth century when women won political franchise through the suffrage movement population growth in European countries has declined. I read a statistic stating the reproductive rate of women of European extraction in North America is 0.72 children per woman; numbers which would put this group on the endangered species list. If every woman on the planet has political franchise, world population will drop to a billion in five generations without any effort.

There is a need to **end war.** Countries are just like people. They want to go about their business without interference. When countries go about their business, the interference between them ,in the absence of law, will cause war. At the present time there is no international law forbidding war. A global participative democracy will have the authority to make a law to end war.

The answer to the question of what would the political system of the future be like ten years after people gave themselves equal political authority is easy to answer? Because there is no need to change any of our political institutions governments would look exactly the same. Politicians will get elected just as they are today. Governments will change about as much as they did when women were given the vote in the early part of the twentieth century. The structure of government and the institutions we see today will remain the same. Governments with the Westminster style of parliamentary democracy will have their prime minister, their cabinets their elected officials and their bureaucracies. Governments like the Constitutional Republic of the United States will have their congress, presidential office and bureaucracies. Government business will proceed as it always has. The difference will be in the respect citizens have for the laws produced by governments.

Change will occur in our communities. With time more and more citizens will want to participate. After a decade or so it will be possible to label new laws and legislations with a level of consensus. This rating over time will become more important and in the end only laws passed with a consensus of citizens will be acceptable. Governments will boast about how their laws are all passed using legitimate authority. In a slow process old laws which were made by representative democracies will be re-examined through the rigors of the legislative process. A fresh new set of laws will be created with known legitimacy. Citizens will get involved in eliminating laws made by our old representative governments that give unearned privilege to individuals or corporations. Necessary laws, (to stop global change and war caused by man) that our representative democracies do not have the authority or the will to pass, will be instituted by a participative government.

Women will be more involved than men and for the first time in history the mass of our women will control the majority of authority to make law in our societies. Under their guidance places will be found for homeless people. Laws judged incentives to crime, (fueling an ethnos) will be eliminated effectively removing the criminal elements from our society. Legitimate businesses or government agencies will provide substances and comfort to the needy while putting the taxes from these enterprises into research and educational programs. Our free market economy will be improved by government legislation taking away the monopolistic privilege taken by established corporations. Real change will come in protecting our environment and reducing our carbon footprint.

Through bureaucratic reduction millions of people, presently working in government offices, will be available to share the workload of maintaining the quality of life in societies. Our news media will be filled with good news stories of how our citizens are moving toward a twenty hour work week with flexible hours. People will have free time to enjoy and strengthen bonds between family and friends and also foster creativity and innovation. Peoples' traits will be nourished as they were in ancient Athens. Natural strengths in sport, intellectual activities, art and philosophy will come forward unrestricted by lack of free time. Women of European extraction will have time to bear children and get off the endangered species list.

New efficiencies will lead to declining taxes and surpluses of money to fuel projects to make our world sustainable.

When things go wrong, people will no longer be able to point a finger and say it's the governments fault. The ownership and responsibility will be in the hands of every citizen. Citizens will change their attitude and work together to build the best, long lasting solutions.

In the past there were many weaknesses in participative democracy. The people of Attica didn't keep a strong enough military to protect their sovereignty. Some say the Golden Age of Athens ended in 403 BC when the Athenian military lost the Peloponnesian war. As noted earlier the democracy in Attica was not a true democracy by modern definition. Women and slaves did not control their POPA. It can be argued that our representative democracy is not a true democracy because modern citizens are equivalent to women and slaves of ancient Greece in that we don't control our POPA between elections.

If the Ancient Greek democracy was such a good thing why did it end? Some would say it never ended. It floundered for a couple of thousand years but never completely died. The seed of democracy re-sprouted with the French Revolution and is now flourishing in Western Society. We need only examine our system of law, public education, the concept of the Olympic Games and the word we all hold so dear, democracy.

The world has never known a true participative democracy. No one can predict with any certainty what the world will be like, however, there is good evidence in our recent past to show the improvements we have had with representative democracy. If the next step from representative democracy to participative democracy produces anything like the shift from the Aristocracy of Europe to a representative democracy the world will be a truly amazing place, with undreamed of peace, love and security.

For millenniums oppressive sources of authority, the aristocracy of Europe and the Roman Church to name a few, have built social constructs based on fear from cosmos and tyranny of the majority or mob rule from the ethnos. Careful reading of the literature indicates the cause of bad tyranny of the majority, (riots and violent uprisings) originates in the vested interest of an ethnos, a ruler, or an oligarchy creating an environment of oppression. History clearly indicates that this threat is completely unfounded in a participative democracy. When we see, in the media, mobs breaking windows and pillaging shops ask yourself what the mothers, the aunties, the grandmothers, all the good men, the uncles and grandfathers think because they will be the ones controlling the making of laws. Tyranny of the majority is impossible in a true participative democracy. Many of the aspects of our successful society have come directly from the study of Athenian participative democracy which some would characterize as tyranny of the majority. The fact that our societies could not exist without the co-operation of our citizens in modern times is an indication that fear of tyranny of the majority is unfounded.

Chapter 23 *Compelling Reasons for Participative Democracy*

Our debt is eroding our social programs, our infrastructure, and our citizen's ability to pay for necessary projects. Our natural resources are being extracted at an ever-increasing rate, and our social structures are decaying into a new form of lawlessness. Plutocrats are inflating property values in our cities to the point that most citizens have become renters with no hope of owning their own home. The good news is we are standing on the top of a mountain and on the other side are valleys filled with hope, and lasting peace. Only the beneficial, sustainable aspects of humanity can fit into this new world by virtue of its system of government.

We live in a representative democracy. There was a reason for this in the past. A hundred years ago representative democracy worked better than the alternatives. Our population was divided into few who were well enough informed, and well enough educated to make viable political decisions. In today's world at least 80 % of us are well enough educated and probably better informed than the best informed of our forefathers. In the past the majority benefited from the spillover of wealth from the wealthy. We can all be thankful for the society that was built in this way. With modern media anyone can be better informed than the leader of a country.

There are strong arguments for participative democracy documented in dozens of books; Benjamin Barber's book "Strong Democracy" and "The Rebirth of Urban Democracy", J. M. Berry, are two good examples. Unfortunately none give a clear guide to accomplishing their goal. They all allude to, but none state that, representative democracy lacks effective feedback mechanisms while sustainable natural systems in our biosphere abound with feedback mechanisms.

A participative democracy is a truly organic system of government controlled by human diversity. Citizen's attitudes will change when we feel ownership and responsibility for the laws which govern our lives. People will begin to trust each other eliminating the need for security. Healthy co-operation, debate, and participation will ensue. This change in attitude is worth a lot. Utilizing citizens in decision-making means more money and a higher quality of life for all people.

There is hope and a reason for optimism. For the last twenty years Western democracies have had the technical ability to run an electronic participative democracy. What would this mean to our populations? When citizens are given an opportunity to participate there will be a large shift in attitude; not only in the people, but also in the politicians and the leaders in society. The blame or credit for making decisions will shift from government, to the total population.

Responsibility in decision-making will cause people to become less apathetic and more involved. It will also end the concealment and dishonesty we see in modern politics, but the biggest benefit will be the direct link between citizens and the political authority of a participative democracy. When leaders in society like Dr. David Suzuki or Al Gore fill our heads with facts about what we are doing to the planet we will judge the facts and have the political authority to make effective laws to fix the problems.

For thousands of years the common man has had little effect on political decision-making. It's like getting enthusiastic about growing a garden, while year after year plants come up only to wither. It's not long before an attitude develops of, "why bother?" If you are having no effect, you don't want to put the effort into gardening anymore. However, just as a gardener who grows a beautiful garden has no shortage of energy, an electorate who finds they have autonomy will have unending energy to find the best solutions to the problems we are facing.

Chapter 24 *Three Challenges*

Throughout history we have had many revolutions. Some start with a spark, (the French Revolution) grew into a searing flame which consumed the past and left death, blood, sorrow, smoke and ash. I am advocating for a green revolution where seeds are planted in the form of ideas that mature over decades of thought. The fruit from these mature trees of understanding will expose the beauty of humanity and fill the future with sweet contentment.

The first challenge: Most universities have political science departments. Political Scientists have a deep understanding of politics. They understand the principles of oppression verses liberty. They understand law is the magic spice holding our societies together. Rather than waiting for some revolutionary force to modernize our political system, I would like the political scientists of the world to formulate some basic principles. The equation, $Q=L/O$ where Q= quality of life. L= Liberty. O=Oppression, needs to be solved. Methods to accurately measure oppression, liberty and quality of life need to be established.

Corporations dilute democratic authority in the absence of political engineering with armies of social engineers, producing well engineered strategies to control the life of our citizens. Our democratically elected governments don't have the political engineers we need to design systems to harvest the wealth of authority from our citizens.

I would like political scientists to lay down the fundamental principles of politics as a foundation for faculties of political engineering. The faculties of engineering will study and formulate ways of eliminating oppression while building an environment of liberty. Political engineers will study jurisdictions and use basic principles of understanding to predict the quality of life based on the amount of oppression versus liberty. The graduates of political engineering programs will be employed by governments to expand the work of electoral officers beyond Election Day.

The backbone of our representative democracy is our electoral system. Our electoral officers are trusted to: uniquely identify citizens, build an electoral role, encourage individuals to participate as candidates or voters, ensure fairness with scrutinizers, have an accessible auditing system, give the citizen anonymity, provide equal access by providing convenient polling places and use the authority of the electoral officer to ensure a level playing field in the competitive struggle between candidates. Using modern tools, Political Engineers will take on the role of electoral officer, serving not just through an election but twenty-four seven, three hundred and sixty five days a year.

Engineering students will learn how to build systems uniquely identifying each citizen, ensuring each citizen has equal access to political systems and how to capture the authority of all citizens without prejudice. The graduates of these faculties will have a solid knowledge of every style of authority. They will understand basic principles of how authority can be captured and used for good or bad.

Undergraduate degrees in Computer Science, Political Science, Behavioral science, Psychology, Philosophy and courses giving the student a broad understanding of the human condition will be an asset.

Our society is like whole milk, very quickly stratifying after elections, forming a thin layer of fat at the top consisting of the same old boys who are in control. The role of political engineer is to homogenize the political authority in society by giving each citizen control over their POPA. Their job is to foster liberty defined as freedom with ownership and responsibility by building roads and bridges of understanding and allowing political authority through consensus to be focused through our governments.

Imagine an earthquake in, say, Haiti. Massive devastation and loss of life; nations of the world send millions of dollars' worth of aid. Amazing amounts of clean water, food, tents for temporary shelter, equipment to rescue people and to find trapped bodies, sniffer dogs. The people of the world open their hearts and do their best to give the effected people an opportunity to rebuild their lives. But is it enough?

What if a nation like Canada, with a French speaking population, sent half a dozen newly graduated political engineers? The engineers would do their job of uniquely identifying each camp citizen. The engineers would create an electoral roll and teach the citizens of the camp how they will be in charge of making new rules and laws using a system of participative democracy. The engineers will know exactly how to divide the people into groups and have them elect representatives. The representatives will listen to the people in their group and represent their ideas at council meetings where an agenda will be formulated. The political engineers know how to produce an accurate list of problems and needs. They solicit people to form groups around possible solutions. They organize free and open debates to find the best ideas to solve problems. The rules formulated come from camp citizens not from administrators. The engineers set up a system where each member can give their consent to the solution they think best through a common vote or perhaps by using an electronic device.

This is the beginning. The engineers leave after firmly establishing participative democracy. When they come back in six months they find a central market place, the beginning of a school. The economics of the camp and the amount of aid money is public knowledge and is controlled by the camp citizens. In a year new houses have been built by the newly trained young men of the camp. The same young men are rebuilding the city using modern building techniques. A decade later the camp is a pleasant community producing high-end garments for a thriving tourist industry. Haiti has embraced participative democracy, has established a strong currency, is well prepared for any future natural disaster and is now one of the most sought after tourist destinations in the Caribbean.

Every political body wanting to make legitimate laws will need a political engineer to find, without prejudice, consensus in the body of citizens in their jurisdiction. This consensus is not only for the election of leaders in our political offices, as we have today, but also for measuring consensus to legitimize laws.

The second challenge: Students in public schools will be indoctrinated with the concepts of participative democracy, just as our present population is indoctrinated with the theory of representative democracy. Each student will know they possess and control, if they should survive to the age of consent, a piece of political authority equal to every other citizen. Just as students learn math and physics from the works of physicists and mathematicians, students will learn the fundamental principles of participative democracy from the works of political scientists. When students are well enough informed and reach the age of consent they will give up their status of sponsored citizens and become full citizens. The new citizens will be capable of running a dispute resolving system and be able to judge law based on interference, oppression and legitimacy. Students will understand their liberty comes from their ownership and responsibility in the four layers of government; local, regional, federal and finally, the world government (UN), which will ultimately govern the biosphere of our planet.

Students will be on a level playing field with social engineers employed by corporations. They will learn about marketing, the art of spin and influence peddling. And just as we teach tolerance to religious and sexual orientation, students will also learn about political equality and their personal role in making law.

Today, graduating from high school is a highly celebrated occasion. In the future the celebration of citizenship will be the biggest celebration in a person's life. Some might think putting the burden of ownership and responsibility for the future of our planet on the backs of our young is unfair. I'm convinced this sentiment is opposite to what our young people are looking for.

At the beginning of the twenty-first century, although our teachers work hard, our public schools have an element of discord. Many students do not want to be in school. Their abilities are unchallenged, and they don't seem to have clear direction. People know there is a problem but the ownership and responsibility for these problems falls not on the directly affected parents and teachers but instead on government agencies.

I am confident teachers and parents in a participative democracy will be able to redesign our public schools filling them with knowing strength, security, positive understanding, and purposeful creativity driven by young people's desire to learn about the world they will inherit. Sir Moses Finley in his book "Democracy Ancient and Modern," notes ancient Athens was free of vandalism. The young men of Athens were more interested in enhancing and building a better world then defacing the world they would inherit. It seems the students of that time didn't have the time or the inclination for such foolish things.

The third challenge is now standing in the wings waiting to happen. Mark Zuckerberg saw a need and had the intellectual tools to build a user controlled platform creating a social network. Mark started a social revolution connecting a billion people. I am confident there is a person or a group of people (perhaps political engineers) who will recognize the need for a political network based on the fundamental principle of **each citizen controlling exactly the same amount of political authority from the age of consent until the end of life.** The political network will give each citizen opportunity to exercise their political will at any time. Unlike a representative democracy where the winner of a political contest takes all, in a participative democracy the citizen controls their POPA from the age of consent until the end of life.

In 2018 I can open an app to find to the price of thousands of corporate stock prices, to the penny. I can find the temperature, the atmospheric pressure, wind velocity and direction and the amount of cloud or precipitation for any GPS location on the planet. There is an app to find out what my neighbor's house is worth. I can find an app that shows maps and the name of every street on the planet. However, there is no app telling me who is using my POPA (piece of political authority) to make law, something in a democracy I own and am responsible for.

At this time in history we don't need to change our governments in any way. I hope governments will keep their noses out of any attempt to build a citizen controlled platform to measure consensus. We don't need to change our electoral system in any way. After an election if the candidate a citizen supported didn't get elected it is a simple matter for the citizen to securely log on to the political network and move their POPA to a candidate who does represent their vested interests. It is not necessary to restrict the number of citizen driven platforms. I am hoping every player i.e., Google, Facebook, Twitter and all social networks will provide this service. Political engineers with the help of citizens will be responsible for auditing and interfacing the results as securely as our banks account our money.

The political network will keep track of the amount of POPA each politician controls. Exact numbers of citizens supporting each bill passed into law using the number of supporters each politician is representing at the time of the vote will give a measure of legitimacy.

The political network will have political influence to begin with and conceivably, if a consensus of citizens wishes it, full political authority sometime in the future.

Chapter 25

Questions and uncertainties

The question remains, if we do utilize our present resources, and form a participative electronic democracy allowing citizens to control their POPA, one can only speculate on the outcome. However, one can take comfort in the writings of the leaders of our past.

Theodore Roosevelt: "The majority of the plain people will day in and day out make fewer mistakes in governing themselves than any smaller body of men will make trying to govern them."

Thomas Jefferson: "I know of no safe depository of the ultimate power of the society, but the people themselves, and if we think them not enlightened enough to exercise their control with a wholesome discretion, the remedy is not to take it from them, but to inform their discretion."

John Stewart Mill: "The greatest dangers of democracy lie in the sinister interests of the holders of power."

Rousseau Jean Jacques: "Man imposes freedom on himself."

Few would argue that modern society exists today because of this ancient anomaly called democracy. The environment of liberty from 508 BC to 198 BC in ancient Greece created a freedom sufficient to allow the scholars of that time to lay the foundation of modern science, medicine, mathematics, philosophy, and politics.

As always, the powerful have used democracy to their advantage with the spill-over benefiting the common people. We have a representative democracy today with the view that competition for leadership, among elites, is the essence of democracy, more important than the laws produced by our governments. Our present prosperity argues favorably for this system. However, as we enter the information age, large cracks are evident in the foundations of our democracy.

Benjamin Barber a Political Scientist in his book, "Strong Democracy" describes a growing potential for pathology in our present thin democracy as our young people become disfranchised in a system increasingly favoring the elite minority.

I know there are power centers in the world that would go against a crusade for participative democracy, however I believe participative democracy is inevitable and a reason for hope. Unlike Ancient Greece we will not exclude any element of our society. Participative democracy does not recognize race, religion, gender, color, status, wealth, or political standing. Participative democracy qualifies participants as human beings with a heat beating in their chest that are of the age of consent.

Of the dozens of books that have been written on the subject of participative democracy, none have a viable system that will work. We have been indoctrinated and have lived with representative democracy for our entire lives, never experiencing anything else. People in our society don't know their past. The fact is, there are no examples of a true participative democracy. The closest mankind has come was in Attica (508 BC to 198 BC). Few would argue that without the anomaly of this radical democracy in Ancient Greece, our society, for better or worse, wouldn't exist today.

The Second reason is a failure of our oligarchies to truly hand over real power to the people. In ancient Athens the Assembly of citizens became the sovereign voice of the state. No one could challenge or alter its decision. The people's decision was final, just as the decision is final when a candidate is elected in a representative democracy. Until this time the rulers of factions held power in Attica. When this power was truly divided equally between each citizen, by (Solon and later Cleisthenes) the rulers of the factions lost their power. They became leaders; leaders that couldn't rule using questionable authority. To be effective within the citizen's assembly these would be tyrants needed to use legitimacy from citizens. This assembly maintained many would-be rulers as leaders. Socrates, Plato, and Aristotle all had aspirations to rule, however they earned immortality as great leaders within this system.

The third reason is size: A century ago we couldn't inform interested citizens, and we couldn't accurately tally all the votes. Today we can get a message to almost everyone in the world within seconds, quicker and more efficiently than the fastest runner across ancient Attica. The world has grown very small, and we now have the equipment to accurately tally all votes with ease and complete security.

Some people think the super-rich can save the world. I think the common people can save the world if we struggle for real political franchise (suffrage to participate). By utilizing the largest resource we have, the majority of our decision makers, we will have a chance to slow down our present momentum and create a new world based on the joy of life with our fellow humans and harmony with all life on this planet.

Our leaders need only have the goals of a sustainable economy, a sustainable social structure, and a sustainable environment, then they must allow the people living in a participative democracy to do the rest.

Because the majority of humans on the planet are women I can see an end to war, a powerful modernization of third world countries and a sharp decline in population growth.

References:

1. Desola Pool, Ithiel "Technologies of Freedom" Cambridge,   Mass.: Harvard University Press. 1983 343.73

2. Finley, M. I. "Democracy: Ancient and Modern" London: Holgarth Press, 1973   321.8

3. Hanna Arendt The Human Condition, 1958.

4. Pateman, Carole, "Participation and Democratic Theory" New York: Cambridge University Press, 1970 321.801

5. 5. Karl Mark & Frederick Engels, The Communist Manifesto, Das KapitaL

6. Adam Smith, The Wealth of Nations.

7. Fox, P. W. "Politics:" Canada Seventh Edition, McGraw -Hill Ryerson, 1991 320.971

8. Churchill, Winston. "A History of the English Speaking Peoples". 4 Volumes , Mew York: Dodd, Mead 1983 942 CH

9. Barber, Benjamin R. "Strong Democracy", Participatory   Politics for a New Age Berkeley University of California   Press 1984 423.B243 c. 1

10. Schumpeter, J. A. "Capitalism, Socialism and Democracy," Geo. Allen & Unwin, London. 1943

11. Samuel Bowles, Herbert Gintis "Democracy & Capitalism",   Basic Books, Inc. New York 1986

12. Adler Mortimer J. "Haves without have-nots" Macmillan   Publishing Company New York 1991

13. Woodcock George "Anarchism and Anarchists" Quarry   Press,   Inc., Kingston, Ontario 1992

14. Miller, James "Rousseau: Dreamer of Democracy" Book Crafters, Inc., Chelsea Michigan. 1984

15. Cross and Woozley "Plato's Republic" Macmillan Company of Canada Toronto. 1964

16. C.E. Robinson "HELLAS" Beacon Press Boston. 1948

17. Berry, Portney, Thompson "The Rebirth of Democracy" THE BROOKINGS INSTITUTION Washington, D.C.

18. Richard Pipes, "Communism A History 2001" modern Library Edition Copyright 2001 by Richard Pipes

19. Leon P. Baradat, Political Ideologies Their Origins and impact Seventh Edition Prentice Hall, Upper Saddle river, New Jersey 07458.

20. Allan Bloom "The Republic of Plato" second edition. Basic Books, Division of Harper Collins Publishers.

21. Gwynne Dyer, Future Tense The coming world order. McClelland & Stewart Ltd. The Canadian Publishers Toronto Ontario.